1982

TWAYNE'S WORLD AUTHORS SERIES

A Survey of the World's Literature

Sylvia E. Bowman, Indiana University

GENERAL EDITOR

FRANCE

Maxwell A. Smith, Guerry Professor of French, Emeritus

The University of Chattanooga
Former Visiting Professor in Modern Languages
The Florida State University

EDITOR

Georges Duhamel

(*TWAS 199*)

TWAYNE'S WORLD AUTHORS SERIES (TWAS)

The purpose of TWAS is to survey the major writers—novelists, dramatists, historians, poets, philosophers, and critics—of the nations of the world. Among the national literatures covered are those of Australia, Canada, China, Eastern Europe, France, Germany, Greece, Italy, Japan, Latin America, the Netherlands, New Zealand, Poland, Russia, Scandinavia, Spain, and the African nations, as well as Hebrew, Yiddish, and Latin Classical literature. This survey is complemented by Twayne's United States Authors Series and English Authors Series.

The intent of each volume in these series is to present a critical-analytical study of the works of the writer; to include biographical and historical material that may be necessary for understanding, appreciation, and critical appraisal of the writer; and to present all material in clear, concise English—but not to vitiate the scholarly content of the work by doing so.

Georges Duhamel

By BETTINA L. KNAPP

Hunter College

Twayne Publishers, Inc. : : New York

To
DANIEL and MORRISON

Preface

A study of Georges Duhamel's literary works is particularly apt today in view of the cataclysmic times we are now traversing. Altered values and concepts have given birth to a spirit of uncertainty, to a climate of extremes, where passions, violence, and materialism have brought civilization, as we know it, to the edge of a gaping abyss. To offset the effect of chaos which not only pervades our society but engulfs the minds and souls of individuals, thereby unleashing frightening amounts of unchanneled energy, one might do well to read the volumes of a man who not only predicted this turn of events but whose personality and words exude the harmony and peace which come from a balanced personality and a fulfilled existence.

Georges Duhamel, whom I had the pleasure of meeting at his home in Paris in 1952, was a man whose entire being radiated calm, sagacity, and infinite compassion for his fellow human beings. Though our conversation centered mainly on theatrical questions, such as his friendship with Jacques Copeau, his own concepts of drama and how these were worked out in his plays, it also encompassed present-day civilization, its reliance upon the machine rather than upon the individual and the robotlike people it was breeding. Every now and then Duhamel would turn to his still very beautiful wife, Blanche Albane, the former actress, and include her in our discussion. No matter what questions were posed or topics pursued, both Georges Duhamel and his wife were gracious in their ways, patient and explicit in their answers, always ready to elaborate when necessary.

The garden where we conversed seemed to reflect the relaxed and tender modulations of Duhamel's inner being. It was set in the back of his home on the Rue de Liège in Paris, protected by a heavy iron gate from the bustle of the outside world. It was here that Duhamel had spent so many hours in fruitful meditation. Now his grandchildren, toddlers at the time, kept running in and out of the house, playing amid the small shrubs and delicate flowers, running toward their grandparents every now and then for a hug or some reassuring words. The warmth and understanding exuded by the Duhamels, not only toward their own flesh and blood—which of course was utterly natural—but toward a stranger, was an indication of their personalities and the manner in which they experienced life.

In this volume on Georges Duhamel I have tried to underscore in his literary works the manner in which a balanced individual such as he views the world and copes with its myriad problems in a rational and humanitarian manner. Duhamel was not spared any of the torments which life so generously dispenses. He knew great poverty as a youngster; he was brought up in an extremely painful parental environment; he experienced gruesome years as a surgeon in the two world wars. But he also knew happiness. He experienced sensations of euphoria when contemplating nature in its various moods, in his relationship with his wife which was ideal, and in his rapport with his three sons, his grandchildren, his friends. Moreover, he experienced fulfillment as both scientist and writer. Duhamel was not a driven man, nor was he at the mercy of any passion or obsession. He had his likes and dislikes, to be sure, since he was a man of firm convictions, but these never forced him into irrational paths.

Duhamel's polemical works are frequently incisive studies concerning aspects of society which he liked or found despicable. A great patriot, an archindividualist, he struggled valiantly in all of his writings (essays and novels) against those forces he felt were at work trying to undermine or destroy man's inalienable right to grow independently and to express himself freely.

Early in the 1920's Duhamel not only foresaw the instability which was to rock our society today but fought as best he could against what he felt was causing this turmoil. The frantic speed with which collectivization in the United States and the world over was taking place acted as a determining factor in destroying individuality and creating a society of identityless beings. Moreover, overreliance on the machine places too little responsibility on the human being. No pleasure is, therefore, taken in what is made or in a job performed: people become functions and are never able to act in a truly creative manner. Since no satisfaction is derived from labors performed, fulfillment is not possible. Frustration, anger, and distress set in—these emotions remain unchanneled.

Politically speaking, Duhamel was against a welfare state. He believed in democracy, in which the individual would labor diligently in his profession or job and be forced to expend *effort* to earn his daily bread.

The state would come to the rescue in needy cases but would not intervene to the great extent it does today, depriving the individual of the stimulus and initiative necessary to grow and to create. Abandon individual effort and incentive, Duhamel said, by granting individuals anything and everything they wish—gratify them at all times—and you will create a society of lethargic entities whose talents will lie fallow and finally wither away. Worse, idleness and boredom create anguish, havoc, anger, and dissatisfaction. There is but one step from this inner void to the traumatic state of bloodshed, crime, and violence.

Duhamel was not only politically but socially oriented. He led virtually a one-man crusade against air pollution in the 1920s. He wrote essays and books on the destruction of the atmosphere by factories. Many in his entourage thought he was exaggerating the point; others were angered; and still others thought his statements were a sign of mental aberration. Duhamel suggested ways and means of sifting the excess odors from factories, the lethal fumes from refining companies, and so on.

Duhamel was equally outspoken against people's addiction to radio, to films, and to what many have since alluded to as the "idiot box," or television. To have both children and adults accept what they see and hear before them is to lull them into a false state of receptivity and relaxation, never giving them a chance to exercise discernment or initiative. Certainly such a state of affairs is not only dangerous in terms of individual development but creates a society of gaping "acquiescers."

In the field of education Duhamel deplored the fact that classical studies and the humanities were lessening in importance. He felt that the study of Latin, for example, was an invaluable aid in training the mind, not only as an exercise, but as a means of forcing the student to think out certain situations logically as well as philosophically. Duhamel was greatly dismayed to learn that people no longer practiced the art of reading. As a youngster and throughout his life, Duhamel was an inveterate reader. Familiarizing himself with the thoughts of the great minds of the past and present gave him immeasurable pleasure and enriched his inner world, his frame of reference, and his concepts. What greater joy is there, he reasoned so frequently, than the treasures one discovers when reading a fine book? Duhamel also advocated conversation, as had Montaigne in the sixteenth century. Since one is forced to listen while the other person airs his ideas, this art—also lapsing into desuetude today—stimulates thought, is a means of communicating with people, and teaches one patience.

Duhamel's philosophy grew and developed with the passing of years.

A pacifist his entire life, he was also a realist. He realized regretfully that certain situations confronting a country require military intervention, as was necessary, for example, in both world wars. Duhamel was nonetheless a firm believer in *rapprochement* with Germany after World War I; when he visited his former enemy, he gave lectures in various universities where he had been invited and tried as best he could to maintain cordial relations with German writers and men of science. After World War II Duhamel was a firm believer in the United Nations and believed that eventually man would come to understand his alikeness—though holocausts might become manifest in the interim. Indeed, he predicted that if countries did not come to some kind of understanding among themselves through the United Nations or some such international organization, East and West could clash with such force that a war of the worlds would come to pass—two opposing philosophies would meet, each attempting to annihilate the other.

Since Duhamel's philosophical outlook altered to a certain extent with the passing of years, I have opted for a chronological approach to the study of his works rather than for a thematic one. I have tried to bring out in this manner the evolution of a man's art and thought as he steps from one stage in his life to another, broaching various problems in different manners.

My thanks to Vernon Brooks for his expert editorial help, and to Professor Maxwell Smith for his suggestions.

One might do well to read Duhamel's works today because they are the expression of a man whose entire view of life was based on integrity, fortitude, and humanity. This does not imply that an attempt to emulate his ways is in order but that the reader may draw strength from his methods, his objective and impassioned views, the clarity of his thought, his scientific and humanitarian manner of dealing actively and constructively with pressing and perplexing situations.

Duhamel was unusual in his day. Today, this type of person is *unique!*

Contents

Chronology

Chronology

1884 Georges Duhamel is born in Paris.
1885 Leaves for Le Havre. Financial plight difficult.
1888 Returns to Paris. Communal school.
1895 Lycée Buffon.
1899- Lycée at Nevers.
1900
1903 Studies medicine.
1904 Travels through Central Europe on foot.
1905 Visits Switzerland, Tyrol, Austria, Italy on foot. Becomes friend of Charles Vildrac, Henri Mondor, René Arcos, Jules Romains, Albert Gleizes, Berthold Mahn, Albert Doyen. Founds l'Abbaye of Créteil.
1907 First poems: *Legends, Battles.*
1908 End of Abbaye venture.
1909 Marries the actress Blanche Albane. Works in laboratory.
1910 Writes the poetry column for the *Mercure de France.*
1911 *The Light,* first play, produced at the Odéon.
1914 Volunteers for the army as doctor aide-major, second class.
1917 Publication of *The New Book of Martyrs.*
1918 Wins the Goncourt Prize for *Civilization.*
1919 Experiences a great success with *The Heart's Domain.*
1920 The publication of *Confession at Midnight,* the first volume of the series entitled *Life and Adventure of Salavin.*
1922 Buys Valmondois property, near Nesles (Seine-et-Oise).
1924 Second volume of the Salavin series to be published: *Two Men.*
1927 *Salavin's Journal.* Travels to Russia.
1928 Travels to the United States. His father dies in Paris.
1929 Fourth volume of the Salavin series: *The Lyonese Club.*
1930 The "Grand Prix de l'Académie française" for *America: The Menace, Scenes from the Life of the Future.*
1933 First volume of the Pasquier chronicles: *The Notary from Le Havre.*
1934 Second and third volumes of the Pasquier chronicles are published: *The Garden of the Savage Beasts* and *A View of the Promised Land.*

1935 Made a member of the French Academy. Fourth volume of the Pasquier chronicles: *Saint John's Eve*. Becomes director of the *Mercure de France*. Maintains this post until 1937.

1937 Elected to the Academy of Medicine. Publication of *The Bièvres Desert* and *The Masters*. Elected president of the Alliance française.

1938 Seventh volume of the Pasquier chronicles: *Cécile Among Us.*

1939 Eighth volume of the Pasquier chronicles: *The Struggle Against Shadows*. Death of Duhamel's mother in Paris.

1940 Election to the Surgical Academy. At Rennes, where he cares for the wounded in a civilian hospital.

1941 Ninth volume of the Pasquier chronicle: *Suzanne and the Young Men*. His book seized and burned by the Germans. The Germans forbid the publication of his books.

1944 Elected to the Academy of moral and political sciences.

1944 Tenth and last volume of the Pasquier chronicle: *Joseph Pasquier's Passion.*

1949- Lectures widely and travels all over the world—to Africa, South
1956 America, Asia, Finland, Japan.

1950 *The Voyage of Patrice Periot* published.

1951- Publishes a whole series of novels and essays, including such
1960 works as *Cry out of the Depths, The Voyagers of Hope, The Archangel of Adventure, Théophile's Complex.*

1966 April 13, Georges Duhamel dies at his home at Valmondois.

CHAPTER 1

"Appetite for life ..."[1]

I *Childhood and Youth*

D UHAMEL'S LIFE WAS one of balance, the result of a concerted effort on his part to create order out of chaos, to transform the irrational into the reasonable, to reconcile the violence and cruelty inherent in nature with its harmonious and peaceful aspects. Duhamel was an idealist, but he was a realist as well. He sought, therefore, to accommodate himself as best he could to the society of which he was a part, struggling ceaselessly to alleviate man's suffering in his capacity both as doctor and as man of letters. He fought valiantly to maintain righteousness and a spirit of integrity in all of his endeavors, whether political, social, or literary. It was Duhamel's extreme compassion for humanity, his ineluctable goodness, his profound understanding of others which made him outstanding in his time—and beloved to so many.

Georges Duhamel was born in Paris on June 30, 1884. His parents, of old peasant stock, originally from the Ile de France region, were determined and forceful people. Because their personalities were so strong, both mother and father, in different ways, played an important part in the youngster's life during those all-too-impressionable early years.

Georges' father, Pierre-Emile, was a bizarre type of individual. Rather quixotic in his habits, he was forever changing jobs (botanist, pharmacist, journalist, businessman, candy salesman, doctor, and so on) as well as domiciles. His family never knew what to expect of him, nor did he really know himself what he would do next. When he was a bachelor such behavior was detrimental to no one; Pierre-Emile could give vent to any and all of his whims and fantasies and suffer few, if any, consequences. As the father of eight children (four of whom died at an early age), his way of life was not a wholesome one. Because he lacked stability, he could not persevere in any one field and, therefore, was

incapable of earning a living. As a result, his family was forever beset
with financial burdens. When, past the age of forty, he decided to study
medicine, his wife and children were stunned. Pierre-Emile received his
medical degree at the age of fifty-one, in 1900. Intellectually and in
terms of his personality, Georges' father was fascinating. No one was
ever bored in his presence. He was an excellent conversationalist, suave
in his ways, ingratiating when he wanted to be. There was another side
to him, however, which his family knew only too well and experienced
with trepidation. Selfish and egocentric, he spent little time with his
wife and children, preferring the company of strangers, who were
perhaps more exhilarating to him, than that of his intimates. Moreover,
he was prone to uncontrollable bouts of rage. Such outbursts account
for the atmosphere of fear and trembling which pervaded the home
each evening when he made his presence known. As a husband with an
eye for other women, Pierre-Emile was a constant source of despair to
his wife.

Duhamel's mother, Emma Pionnier, was an attractive, intelligent,
and gentle woman. She was endowed with all those remarkable
characteristics one associates with a "perfect-mother" type and for
which all children long. Always guided by her heart, she knew
instinctively how to treat people, help the needy and neglected, and
dispense tenderness and compassion at the proper moments. Infinitely
understanding of her husband's aberrations, she was always ready to
forgive, and she believed fervently that good would win out. Once,
however, when the pain she experienced at her husband's infidelities
was too great, she attempted suicide. After this incident, she accepted
her solitude—her fate—and tried to fill the void in her heart through
frenetic activity. She was busy from dawn till dusk attending to
housework and devoting her time to her children, guiding them into
fruitful occupations. It could be asserted that Madame Duhamel was a
stoic of sorts. When she lost her four children, she withstood the agony
by burying her pain. Madame Duhamel was a practical woman. She did
not live in a dream world. She could not. Her husband's irrational
behavior frequently forced her to face difficulties alone. The onerous
task of moving, for example, was always placed on her shoulders; the
lack of money was her preoccupation; it was she who had to make ends
meet, to care for the children when they were sick, to attend to their
schooling. Despite her pressing problems, Madame Duhamel was always
vigilant concerning the needs of others. Jealousy and anger were not

characteristic of her. Life was accepted in its traumatic and in its beautiful moments.

One can easily understand why the young Duhamel so loved his mother and responded to the warmth she dispensed, why he resented and disliked his father. The constant shifting of domiciles imposed upon the family by the father was not only unpleasant and difficult but created psychological havoc; the changing of jobs made for further insecurity, as did the paucity of funds and the father's temper, which instilled fright in every member of the family. The series of mistresses left an indelible mark of disgust on Georges. In his own life, the lad perhaps unconsciously sought to be the opposite of his father: steady in his studies, considerate of others, realistic in his attitudes.

In his autobiography *Light on My Days (Lumières sur ma vie)*, Georges Duhamel tells us that he was a sickly child. It seems that his spinal column was weak, and because of this disability the doctors had ordered him to sleep on a hard mattress and had also suggested frequent sea baths.[2] He recalls with horror other occasions, when his mother took him to the slaughterhouse in Paris, also at the doctor's request, and there, among the squealing and bleating of the doomed sheep and cows, he was forced to drink their "hot blood" from a cup handed to him. His early school days were equally gruesome. Since he had to receive special care, the boy had led a relatively sheltered existence. He was, therefore, fearful of the outside world, and contact with strangers—even those his own age—was cause for alarm. When first in school, Duhamel wrote, he felt like a small fish in a gigantic ocean. There were always other students, stronger and more vigorous than he, who tyrannized him, made fun of him because he was small, weak, and (to make matters worse) myopic. His schoolmates were forever punching and fighting with one another, whereas he retreated, preoccupied mostly with his own personal problems. Even at this early age, he informs us, he was a pacifist type, convinced that violence was not and would never be the supreme manipulator of destinies. Reason was Duhamel's motivating force rather than coercion; conversation rather than anger. He tried, therefore, to understand and to reconcile two conflicting universal ways: peace and harmony which he sought to establish in his own life and in the world about him, and strife and aggression on an earth filled with "animals of prey."[3]

Though Duhamel's mother was a devout Catholic and tried to inculcate her son with her beliefs, Georges lost his faith at about the age of thirteen. He was an agnostic and remained one his entire life. To adhere to the laws imposed upon an individual by the church would have been hypocritical on his part. To live by his own moral credo—which included kindness, gentleness, a desire to better man's lot and to help others—would be Duhamel's way of life.

Whether Duhamel's love for mankind developed his profound sense for nature or the latter brought forth the former is a moot question. Duhamel's artistic nature and his emotions found an outlet in the forces he saw growing, burgeoning, and dying about him. When very young, during his adolescence, and throughout his mature years, he experienced both joy and an extreme sense of repose while walking and running through open fields and swamps, camping out at night, or merely observing animal life—even frogs jumping about him in a large expanse of greenery. The various odors of the fields—hay, vineyards, flowers in bloom, vegetables growing—warmed by the sun or chilled by the frost, capitvated his senses. Nature's immense variety of colors stimulated his esthetic self: the rhythms of the trees and shrubs swaying in the wind, forever altering their patterns and outlines as they jutted forth, sharply or in rounded shapes, into the horizon. Whether nature was cultivated or merely grew freely, willy-nilly Duhamel experienced a profound affinity with its forces on both a spiritual and physical level.

Duhamel's love for nature did not preclude his passion for Paris. He found pleasure wandering through its maze of crooked, straight, and curving streets, peering into a variety of curiosity shops, or walking up the Montmartre hill with its charming frame houses and its frequently seedy cabarets and small theaters; or strolling along the Seine, poring over the many bookstalls which contained fascinating works of art as well as priceless volumes. Duhamel also made a habit of going to historic museums or to private homes, to theaters, and to concerts. He experienced Paris as a living entity which injected him with life and to which he gave life.

All facets of existence inspired Duhamel. Music, for example, afforded him extreme joy. He played the flute very well and had a remarkable memory for melodies. Indeed, he wrote in his autobiography that if he once heard a tune or aria, he could remember it for over forty years.[4] As a child, he went to the opera and to concerts whenever he could save a few sous. He was enthralled by such works as Berlioz, *The Damnation of Faust*. Later, in his more mature years, he was spellbound whenever Mozart and, most particularly, Bach was played: "I discovered a world, that of Bach, a marvellously creative mind, and, if I may say, wonderfully architectural . . . and yet a human mind, a human heart whose charity to me was and remains inexhaustible."[5] If Duhamel was particularly distressed he often played or hummed a melody from Bach, from one of his cantatas, and calm inevitably set in. Music, for Duhamel was life, as important to him for his subsistence as food or air. "It's by means of music, the azure door, that we emerged from true poverty, that of the soul. It is sovereign music that permitted us to perceive the true dimensions of man."[6] Frequently Duhamel worked out his own personal problems through music, first relaxing as he heard the tonal modulations and rhythmic patterns, then sufficiently at ease to gather his thoughts together and seek a logical solution to whatever was plaguing him.

The theater also beckoned Duhamel. As children he and his brother went to the Odéon almost every Thursday and Sunday afternoon. They sat in the "peanut gallery" and were mesmerized by the "fabulous" scenery, the richly costumed stars, the melodramatic plays which kept them inevitably at the edge of their seats, breathless and for hours on end. The "mystery" and the "marvels" set before them on stage captured their imaginations.

Duhamel was also an inveterate reader. He enjoyed the process of learning. Because of such a bent, he spent many hours at his desk studying, the classics mainly. A fine student, endowed with a penetrating and intuitive mind, he decided early in life that he would make his way as a literary man—and also as a scientist—a doctor. This dual interest did not cause serious conflicts within him. He would serve both métiers, if he could, and as efficaciously as possible. He did just that. When literature became a necessity for him, he abandoned an *active* scientific career.

Duhamel received his baccalaureate degree at the age of seventeen. He then studied philosophy and, after this hurdle was passed, worked as a lawyer's clerk. In this capacity, as in all else, he proved to be punctual and conscientious.[7] He did not consider his work intriguing, however, since it consisted mainly of copying various texts and briefs.

At eighteen, Duhamel decided to live away from his parents and become more or less independent. The year 1902, therefore, marks the year of Duhamel's "liberation." Together with two of his friends he rented a room, not very elegant, of course, but adequate, or so he thought, for his needs.[8] After a while, he discovered that inconveniences were forever cropping up in sharing an apartment, even with young men of his own age. He preferred the privacy of living alone. He felt this next step was important for both his growth and development, and should be taken speedily. He moved into his own quarters on the Rue Saint-Jacques. His mother gave him a few sticks of furniture; he bought some himself; and his room was furnished. His living conditions were Spartan, to say the least. Nevertheless, the difficulties arising from the lack of comforts were quickly overlooked, as the pleasures he experienced from the solitude and independence he now enjoyed were extreme. After all, he wrote, "the human world was rich, even in its poverty."[9]

The year 1902 also marked another momentous event for the young man. The very summer he moved into his own lodging he took the first of what were to become many walking trips through France, Switzerland, Austria, Italy, and Germany. Duhamel always had a taste for traveling, which he kept throughout his life. He liked to learn from other people, to become familiar with the variety of philosophies, mores, personalities, and ways of existing in the world. Only through travel could he see man in his environment and observe him.

Duhamel began his medical studies in 1903, two years after his own father had been graduated. The young lad worked arduously throughout medical school, doubly so, since he followed his father's advice and went almost daily to the hospitals to observe a variety of operations, absorbing, thereby, as much as he could in his field of interest. The schedule he set for himself was perhaps too strenuous for his not too strong body. He became run down and, in April 1904, was taken very ill with rheumatic fever. His father diagnosed his sickness almost immediately upon seeing his son return home one afternoon. He cared for him with unstinting devotion, tenderness, and mastery. The young medical student had perhaps never known this side of his father; the discovery was to enrich his own existence and to make him more understanding of his father's complex personality. Duhamel's convalescence took some time. He could not resume his medical studies immediately and was obliged to spend the summer in the country with his friends.

Because Duhamel did not want to rely upon his parents for financial aid, at least not completely, he decided to give French lessons to Russian students flowing into Paris. Since he also had a creative bent, he applied for a part-time job writing articles for a medical encyclopedia. As the years passed he began substituting for doctors who went on vacation or who were otherwise occupied. It seems that all of this activity was not sufficient to tire the energetic Duhamel. His interest in science was so keen he decided to take some extra courses at the Biological Institute.

Science alone, however, did not quench his thirst for knowledge. At this point, literature and poetry mostly seemed to arouse his sensibilities and answer a need within him. He had, at the time, few friends with whom he could discuss literary matters, but this void in his life was soon to be filled, and by chance. One day, while strolling through the Luxembourg Gardens in Paris, he chanced to meet a young man, also walking, who had a very poetic mien about him. His curly hair, his black dolman, his handsome face gave him a rather dashing look; he resembled those Musset-like poets of the nineteenth century. Who would have guessed that this gentle-faced, sensitive-looking man was Charles Vildrac, future essayist, playwright, and poet? A long-lasting friendship flowered from this meeting. Indeed, Vildrac later married Duhamel's sister.

II   *The Créteil Venture*

Vildrac's love for humanity was on a par with Duhamel's. His understanding of poetry was equally profound and quite similar. Each considered Baudelaire and Rimbaud to be his gods. Both young men loved to converse, to air ideas, to stimulate the thought processes. They also believed they had a message which they felt compelled to communicate to society. Duhamel noted in his autobiography, *Light on My Days,* that Vildrac was prone to escapism and melancholia; despite this, he was a passionate human being. Vildrac agreed with Duhamel's appraisal of him and even confessed: "I understand only passion. Passion excuses everything."[10] His plays *Le Paquebot Tenacity (The Steamer Tenacity)* (1920) and *La Brouille (The Quarrel)* (1930), which knew such success the world over, attest to this character trait.

It was Vildrac who first had the idea of establishing an "ideal" communal colony, where young poets would learn a trade in order to become economically independent, then spend all of their free time in creative pursuits. Vildrac had searched assiduously for the "perfect" location for what he was to call his "Abbaye." He found it at Créteil, a beautifully wooded area seven kilometers from Paris, on the shore of the Marne River. There, amid a beautiful park filled with all sorts of plants and a variety of birds, stood a two-story frame house with green shutters and a brown roof. This "dream house," as Vildrac referred to it, had remained uninhabited for several years. Though the plaster was crumbling and the paper on the walls was coming off and not one door

closed properly, Vildrac, Duhamel and the friends they had persuaded
to join them were highly enthusiastic.[11]

Charles Vildrac, René Arcos, the future novelist, Albert Gleizes, the
painter, Henri Martin-Barzun, an essayist and critic-to-be, and Duhamel
signed the lease in 1905. They decided to emulate Rabelais by declaring
that all bigots, everyone hostile to joy and to individual undertakings
would be barred admittance to their home. Each of the participants of
the "Abbaye" venture, as the young men now alluded to it, would
bring all of their enthusiasm with them upon their arrival and also
whatever material possessions they could get hold of. Duhamel brought
an old bed; Vildrac a piano and other furniture; Albert Doyen, an
organ. Each young man would work part time, then be free to practice
whatever art he chose.

Vildrac hired a printer and a press so that the members of the
"Abbaye" could learn to set type and be responsible for the printing of
several books. Duhamel wrote, years later, that he had become so adept
at the printing trade that he could "set" twelve hundred letters an
hour. He enjoyed the feel of paper, the fact that he was working with
his hands. The practicing of a trade gave him indescribable pleasure and
certainly bore out Jean-Jacques Rousseau's counsel, encouraging all
people to perform some kind of manual labor.

The members of the group worked hard at first. They printed the
books of some well-known authors, such as Paul Adam and Anatole
France, who looked with favor upon their venture and tried to help
them as best they could. They also printed their own writings, since
most commercial firms had decided it would be economically unsound
to bring out editions of works by unknown authors. Romains' *La Vie
unanime (Unanimistic Life)*, Vildrac's *Images and Mirages*, Duhamel's
Legends, Battles (Des Légendes, des batailles) were all printed at the
Abbaye.

During working days the members of the colony wore old clothes
and wooden shoes and sometimes shocked the "bourgeois" neighbors
who looked askance at what they considered peculiarities. Duhamel's
own particular situation, however, varied from the rest of the group. He
worked at the Abbaye, to be sure, but he also commuted to Paris daily
to medical school and to the Biological Institute. Life was exciting,
filled with novelty and fecundity. Duhamel was growing intellectually,
emotionally, and socially.

On holidays, the group frequently had musicals and art exhibits.
Friends would come and visit and a merry time was had by all. Luc

Durtain, who nourished literary ambitions, was a frequent visitor to the Abbaye on Sundays mostly, as were the poet Pierre Jean Jouve, the musician Albert Doyen, the painter Berthold Mahn, and the one to receive the greatest recognition of all in the not-so-distant future, Jules Romains.

There is no question but that Charles Vildrac and Georges Duhamel had been influenced by Romains's "unusual" philosophy called "unanimism." The author of the famous play *Doctor Knock* (1923) and the series of novels entitled *Men of Good Will* (1932–47) was both forceful and imaginative. His philosophy was based on the theory that the group was of prime importance and that the individual, especially the poet, can attain power and significance only by merging himself with a social aggregation of one kind or another, he himself being far less important than the collective whole.

Unlike the followers of unanimism, however, each member of the Abbaye group pursued his artistic endeavors individually, never bowing to public or commercial tastes. The members of the Abbaye could, therefore, enjoy the pleasures of remaining masters of their thoughts and concepts, benefiting, at the same time, from effective solidarity.

Life was difficult. The young men, so idealistic, so fervent in their beliefs, had to face the fact that money was scarce. During the winter months they could afford to heat only one room. Fortunately, their taste in food was simple; they ate the most primitive type of nourishment. Despite their enthusiasm for the arts, disagreements among them began to arise. Artists, to be sure, are temperamental types. Though they may try to live out their dreams, when it comes to realizing them on a material level, practicality, *bonhomie* is usually lacking. The Abbaye group was for the most part made up of introverted individuals trying to live under one roof. Resentment, disquietude began to arise. A lack of self-discipline led to quarrels and misunderstandings. Vildrac felt the antagonisms, both latent and overt. He suffered deeply because of the innuendos, the satiric and ironic remarks made by one of his friends to another. Though deeply affected, Vildrac and Duhamel both kept their faith in the group and in humanity. As the months passed, however, their illusions were shattered. They could not reconcile themselves to the fact that intelligent, poetic, and sensitive young men would lose their dignity and fight among themselves as they were doing. The group's noble ideas, the cult of the mind which Vildrac had tried to further, the esthetic sense which he thought would prevail—all vanished.

Créteil was no longer the paradise the young poets and artists had envisaged. It had been transformed into an inferno of hatreds and anger. Creative spirit cannot flourish in an atmosphere replete with discord and base conceptions. Gone were the beauties of nature, the profound desire for solitude and meditation. A maze of unpleasant-nesses, of sordid views had replaced them. The Abbaye de Créteil group disbanded in 1908. Each member thenceforth went his own way.

In Duhamel's case, however, one cannot consider the Abbaye venture as unproductive. It taught him that the realm of the "ideal" was not always the land of the "real," that people, though talented and brilliant, find it hard to work with one another, that man is essentially a gregarious animal, that manual labor has sure reward. Most of all he realized that each being, though he must try to work with his fellow man, must become an entity unto himself: self-sufficient, emotionally speaking, and intellectually independent.

Little change had taken place in Duhamel's scholarly situation. He pursued his medical studies, continued his labors in the laboratory and the hospital. In 1908 he was awarded his degree, *Licence ès sciences.* The following year he received his medical degree, published his second volume of verse, *Man at the Head (L'Homme en tête)* and experienced one of the most momentous events in his life—he married the beautiful and charming aspiring young actress, Blanche Sistoli, whose stage name was Albane.

Duhamel had met Blanche at the Abbaye where she had been a frequent visitor on Sundays and holidays. She loved to listen to the music that was played there, and she enjoyed the country walks and the entire atmosphere which had been created in the early days of the venture. In his autobiography, Duhamel declares that he fell in love with her the moment they met. Her inner beauty, the flow of her gentleness radiated about her always. She was in every sense of the word Duhamel's life companion and though the early days of their marriage were difficult, financially speaking, the depth of their relation-ship, the complete entente between them, was never marred, but grew increasingly more profound. They had three sons as time went on, two of whom became doctors, the third a composer. These sons brought fulfillment to their love.

To support his wife at the outset of their marriage Duhamel found employ in an industrial laboratory doing research work on animals. When he returned to his apartment in the evening, he spent a great deal of his time writing. There were really no conflicts in his life at this time;

his world seemed to be taking its beautiful and rational course. He had patience and perseverance, and he realized that he would have to earn his subsistence in this fashion until he could make his literary works lucrative. Duhamel possessed faith in his own ability.

III A Bout with Poetry

Duhamel had begun writing poetry at an early age, at the Lycée. His verses seemed to flow forth, effortlessly. He himself printed his first volume *Legends, Battles (Des Légendes, des batailles)* (1907), at the Abbaye. This slim book suffers, as is to be expected in an initial poetic endeavor, from a variety of defects, especially a lack of *maîtrise* in technique and undeveloped thought. The poems lack originality and seem to be modeled too strictly upon those in vogue at the time. The preface displays little understanding of the works of such writers as Paul Verlaine and Francis Jammes, to mention only two. One cannot overlook the conceit or youthful brashness which are not only present but are obvious and quite disconcerting at times. These literary traits are absent in Duhamel's later works.

Though Duhamel was doing a lot of writing at this juncture in his life, his ideas had not yet coalesced. They were still disparate, and he was groping. His theories concerning verse, for example, were molded on the poetry of his contemporaries or the ideas of the symbolists. In *Notes on Poetic Technique (Notes sur la technique poétique)* (1910), a volume he coauthored with Charles Vildrac, a marked improvement over his first literary attempt was noticeable. In *Poetic Technique,* a type of "ars poetica," the authors speak in favor—and unequivocally— of free verse. Artificial and forced rhyme schemes, they decided, should be eliminated; alliterations, caesuras, assonances, subtle but never contrived rhymes should add enrichment to poetry. Duhamel and Vildrac attacked conventional verse makers with the authority and confidence of youth: that is, mercilessly. They suggested a variety of rhythmic patterns, intertwining images, various musicalities and balance in poetic endeavors. Each time a certain figure of speech, rule or rhyme was suggested, they illustrated their point with examples drawn from the poetry of René Arcos, André Salmon, Gustave Kahn, Rimbaud, Verlaine, Jammes, Jacob, and others.

Duhamel meanwhile was gaining in self-assurance. An inveterate reader, he would usually take notes when interested in a particular subject, then meditate upon what he had just learned. Moreover, he was always in contact with two different worlds, that of the scientist and that of the literary man. He absorbed the best of each, enriching his own inner domain. When Alfred Vallette, the editor of the *Mercure de France,* one of the outstanding literary magazines of the time, asked him to write the column "Les Poèmes," Duhamel, needless to say, was thrilled. It meant a slowing down of his laboratory work, remuneration for his literary labors.

Vallette and his wife Rachilde deserve special attention not only because they were the editors of one of the most powerful literary magazines but because they became Duhamel's lifelong friends. Indeed, he declared that he never made an important decision in his life without consulting them first.[12]

Vallette and Rachilde represented an era: that of the publisher who encourages little-known writers in whom they have faith. They were a dedicated couple in their approach to art. Because they published manuscripts in which they believed, and overlooked the material aspect of their endeavors, they could not and would not consider themselves commercial publishers. They earned little, therefore, and Vallette took barely enough money to pay for the most minimal of expenses. In the small offices which he and his wife occupied, there was no electricity, no telephone, and hardly any heat at all, even during the winter months. Vallette wanted to spend as little money as possible on his personal needs and invest it all in what he considered of eternal value—his magazine. As a result of his perseverence and Spartan dedication to his principles, he drew many writers of distinction into his fold: Alfred Jarry; Remy de Gourmont, the literary critic of the symbolist school; Paul Léautaud, the novelist who wrote under the pseudonym Maurice Boissard; Guillaume Apollinaire; and a host of others.

Duhamel met many poets, critics, and novelists through Vallette. He became rather friendly with Apollinaire and spent many an evening with him and his friends on the terrace of some Montmartre café or *bistro* on the Faubourg Saint-Antoine, discussing both literary and gastronomical subjects. One evening Apollinaire invited him to spend some time at the home of le Douanier Rousseau, the primitive painter who was to receive such high praise with the passing of years. It was on this occasion that Blanche Albane recited poetry, that Marie Laurencin sang old French songs.

By 1912, Duhamel had amassed a sufficient number of essays and literary criticisms to publish them in volume form. *Critical Remarks (Propos critiques)* contains articles on Rimbaud, analyzing his work, its intensity, beauty, and power, which Duhamel felt most keenly and on Mallarmé, whose secretive, hermetic world of analogies was not as clearly understood by Duhamel and about whom he was, therefore, less analytical. Duhamel was seemingly unable to penetrate Mallarmé's arcane world of breathtaking images and harmonies. Verhaeren's rhythmic verses, which poetized cities and ports, the excitement and noises of the machine age, were more readily discernible to Duhamel and, for this reason, were extremely well described and analyzed. Jammes, the bard of nature whose metaphysical searchings led him to a profounder understanding of the cosmos and of God, was a poet whose work Duhamel also felt clearly and keenly. Other essays in this volume touched upon the romantic symbolist poet Paul Fort as well as others of varying schools: Vielé-Griffin, Romains, Vildrac, Arcos, Chennevière, Paul Claudel.

Duhamel so admired Claudel that the following year he wrote an entire book on Claudel's poetry and theatrical endeavors. For Duhamel poetry had to trace or sear a pathway through life, introduce readers to unknown realms and dimensions. Claudel's verse did just that. "He forces us to throw our old scales and compasses to the wind. . . ."[13] Claudel was, in Duhamel's opinion, the instigator of a new kind of lyricism. Rejecting old and worn metaphors, he injected energy and life into what had been considered antagonistic images and feelings. In this fashion, he introduced the senses to new feelings, extraordinarily beautiful and poignant tones which stirred, distressed, and soothed the reader. "One feels the universe being carried forth in a vast whirling round which is forever renewing life's aspects without ever taking from that devouring past, that event which is never again to be reborn."[14] Claudel's exuberance and vitality, his pain and hatred, his sense of culpability, his anger fill the reader with vertigo. It is like mounting a steep rock, Duhamel wrote, and looking about at the horizon—the open spaces surrounding one.[15] Claudel's powerful poetic voice cascaded forth at every instant, opening up hitherto mysterious realms, bringing forth from these recesses troubled characters which are neither situated in time nor in space, as we look upon these entities. Claudel's writings infuse the innocent reader with passion and life, inflict him with zest.[16]

For Duhamel, Claudel had forged new paths in poetry, most specifically. He had liberated verse from the constraints imposed upon it by rules and regulations. Claudel's images were spontaneous and subjective, bursting forth from each line with the violence inherent in the poet's very soul, with the cruelty and fervor present in his supremely mystical and religious gropings. Each word, refurbished by Claudel, fermented continuously, bubbled over, lived a life of its own, taking on new qualities every second of its life, new and varied intonations and vigorous rhythms—then shot forth, illuminating everything in its path.

Poets and Poetry (*Les Poètes et la poèsie*) (1915), which Duhamel published a year after his volume on Paul Claudel, was more comprehensive in that it evaluated the works of several poets. Duhamel was intent upon writing about well-known poets, as well as those of lesser reputations in the literary field. Biographical notations were therefore included; then an examination of the writings of each of the poets who came under his scrutiny. He endeavored all the while to explain the ideas embedded in their poetry and his opinion concerning the eventual role their works would play in the literary world.

Rimbaud, Duhamel points out, had a prodigious sense of language; he was a savage genius. He created rapid, brutal, pure and luminescent verse. Mallarmé's output, on the other hand, was more reasoned, tempered always by a lucid brain. He sought smaller audiences and was forever clothing his ideas in words possessing mysterious affinities. Verhaeren's natural richness in describing the teeming cities, the bustle of people and machines, perpetual motion and syncopated rhythms can be appreciated most readily by people inhabiting a metropolis, Duhamel intimated. He had a real understanding for Jammes's attitudes toward nature. The poet's descriptions of wheat fields, for example, of the green marshes, the vineyards were both sensual and spiritual and were savored totally by Duhamel. In the essay devoted to Jules Romains, Duhamel endeavored to explain the meaning and value of unanimism in his world. It must be noted that Duhamel's essay on Apollinaire was limited. He failed to recognize this poet's individual talent, the musicality and airiness of his verse. He compared his poems and their imagery to "a store dealing in secondhand goods," so filled was it with disparate objects. Instead of letting himself be guided by the sway and beauty of the lines, Duhamel tried to reason Apollinaire's verse and could not, thereby, be seduced by the ineluctable series of images and intricate rhythmic patterns which would have lulled and swayed him about. Moreover, it would seem that Duhamel was resentful of Apollinaire's work. He felt that the series of words the poet introduced into his verses were virtually meaningless. These afforded the reader clever, but arbitrary and certainly not sincere, sensations. In the last analysis, Duhamel was convinced that Apollinaire's verses were contrived. He was totally oblivious to Apollinaire's auditory patterns, the visual beauty of his stanzas.

Duhamel had not only become a critic, but a poet in his own right. His own verse, which he wrote during his early years (1906–9), appeared in a volume entitled, *Man at the Head (L'Homme en tête)* (1909), which he dedicated to Charles Vildrac.

No matter what type of literary work Duhamel indulged in, whether poetry, short stories, or essays, he always adopted a point of view, a philosophical concept. *Man at the Head,* though strictly poetry, is a case in point. He has not only opted for a definite story line but has created a type of allegory of man's life on earth. Duhamel's hero type in *Man at the Head* is a man, or Anthrope, as he is called, who is a leader of people, a creative being with vision and wisdom. Such a theme is far from original. The Romantic poets throughout the nineteenth century, including Hugo, Vigny, and Lamartine, all believed that the poet's function in society was that of a "messiah," a chief, who is inevitably misunderstood, hurt deeply by society's callous reactions to his words and thoughts. Yet he struggles on and finally emerges victorious.

Duhamel's character, Anthrope, suffers this same fate, that of the pain and disappointment of the visionary who believes in his ideal and who tries desperately to illuminate the masses. Rather than enlighten them, however, he must bow down to them, abandon his own destiny, and become one of many—"The heavy flocks with men's faces." Before Duhamel, the Parnassian poet, Leconte de Lisle, had also spoken of the ugly face of the masses, incapable of understanding the higher philosophical and esthetic points of view. The poet must choose, Duhamel reasons. If he associates with the masses he may be submerged, overpowered by their concerted strength and intrinsic ignorance. If he rejects humanity he will be left to die, alone, misunderstood, rejected. The poet, therefore, withdraws, momentarily at least, from society in order to meditate. He begins to experience the agonies of solitude. He looks with desperation toward nature which he has always considered to be an inarticulate world, physically appealing but essentially hostile. Now, however, his loneliness forces him to touch the flowers, the leaves, the trees and to view their extraordinary beauty. Now he begins to experience nature as something helpful, consoling, understanding, similar to a woman in many respects—tender and beautiful, a force capable of bringing peace within his being. Again the poet looks wistfully toward society. This time he realizes he cannot impart his ideas, his feelings of generosity, to the masses; they are overwhelmed with greed, ignorance and the crassness of materialism. Yet, upon closer scrutiny Anthrope is aware that certain beings do stand out from the madding crowd, do suffer anxiety as he does and are equally dissatisfied with their lot. They too are concerned and just as despairing as the Man at the Head. These beings will be attracted toward the poet and though his message may not be readily understood by them in tone, the fire of his language will persuade them. They will resist the collective leveling which comes with mass acceptance of any idea, mass subservience and mass-produced images. Though few and far between, these exceptional beings strive to uplift themselves, to struggle forth and arise as individuals. Like the poet, they too will be mocked, scoffed and jeered at. At the end of the volume, the poet looks within his own life, and realizes that he does not want to turn toward the madding crowd, or to suffer the pain of solitude. As his thoughts take root, Anthrope suddenly becomes aware of his utter isolation, his solitude has become a negative entity. Nothing fruitful can come to pass from such loneliness; two or more are required for creativity. One being alone—vegetates. Man is essentially a gregarious animal and must work with others. Anthrope, however, makes one more effort to impart knowledge to his fellow men. They are unprepared to receive it. Having failed in this last attempt, Anthrope withdraws to his world of isolation, contemplation—there to vegetate. He turns his back on society in order to live out his own pathetic destiny.[17]

Duhamel's second volume of verse, *According to My Law (Selon ma loi)*, including poetry written from 1909 to 1910, was dedicated to Blanche Albane. Once again he takes up the theme of the poet. His approach this time is less pessimistic. He displays an attempt to reconcile the desire to remain an individual and yet to maintain some kind of contact with man in general. The antagonism for the masses inherent in *Man at the Head* is less pronounced. *According to My Law* begins with a melodious and tender "prelude," in which Duhamel writes:

> Since I shall carry a fate, mine
> Since I shall try my strength, my limits,
> And play the role which belongs to me,
> May energy be given me along with love!

The poet, Duhamel now reasons, cannot live alone. In order to live a positive and fruitful existence, he must enrich his own world through contact with others. He must experience in all ways: suffer, enjoy, and act. If contact is not made with others, the stimulation or energy needed for the creative activity is lacking and, therefore, man's divine half cannot be aroused. A glance, a word, an insignificant detail may permit one being to understand another, may open the door to a *rapprochement* between individuals. Leaders, as well as the masses, must try at least to understand one another, to be gracious in their attitudes, and not always to express their feelings through hatred and bloodshed. If one looks within, Duhamel implies, whether into self or into another being's innermost recesses, one can discover beauty. The search and attempt must be made until the discovery of man's godly side has been accomplished, until the treasure within each creature has been unearthed. Man permits himself, Duhamel continues, to be guided all too frequently by preconceived notions; judgments, therefore, are marred, attitudes of hatred aroused, grievances eternal. Under the guise of such sentiments man becomes powerless to alter relationships and, therefore, veers from one destructive incident to another. Duhamel rejects this kind of attitude based on superficial knowledge of mankind, on egocentric attitudes, and suggests that each creature, through knowledge of self and of others, try—though the task may be difficult—to uplift the masses and impose a new law upon them—a law based on the heart and the mind.

In *The Companions* (*Compagnons 1910-1912*), Duhamel's third volume of poems in this series, he accepts the turmoil of life. Whatever lives in nature, he continues, in the cosmos, has been created by God. Man is the most noble of the divine's creatures and nature is great because it has given birth to man. *The Companions* could be called a type of song or hymn to nature—a pantheistic document in which all that is verdant is viewed from an infinite variety of aspects. Duhamel's vision of the world is grandiose, frequently like Claudel's in that he has expanded his breadth, encompassed a panoramic view as well as a detailed study. Once nature has been experienced as a vital force in life, once man has been understood, life can be lived. Duhamel has little patience for those who dwell in the past or even in the future. One must face the present, he declares with gusto, be vigilant, courageous and sensitive to each event with which one is confronted daily. One must, furthermore, be strong and reject an invasion by the collective, try to understand this phenomenon and relate to each individual as best one can without ever compromising one's personal attitude. Above all, each human being must develop his own way and ideas, his own talents, and profit from the solitude and isolation offered him; if these are not carried to extremes they can be fruitful. Each thinking being must try to guide others and to learn constantly from the world about him.

His *Elegies* (1920), which includes twenty-five elegies and four ballads, is a summing up of what Duhamel had previously stated. Life must be lived fully; it cannot be experienced unless each event and episode—known both intuitively and materially—is accepted as part of daily existence. The riches possessed by each individual can, through contact, be assimilated by others to a certain degree, using meditation as the device permitting such a breakthrough. The world is filled with excitement and myriad riches and these can be possessed through observation, understanding, love, perseverance, and humility. Happiness, which is the goal of existence, can be known throughout one's life on earth, through contact with others and, most deeply, through the creation of the work of art. Happiness, however, is not a condition of stasis. It must be won and it takes effort to win it. It evolves. What brings joy at one period may not at another; inner growth alters attitudes, relationships, desires, and beliefs.

> I gave up many a dream
> To love another,
> And I exchanged, without regrets,
> A thousand lives for one alone.

Though Duhamel always had a soft spot for the art of poetry, he realized that his talents lay elsewhere, in prose. He was not certain, however, what field of endeavor he would choose: the theater? novel? criticism? philosophy? polemics? the short story? or all of them? He was still groping as a writer, and for this reason he was to venture into several areas of literary activity, in an attempt to experience creativity fully and to embed his ideas within his prose in the most incisive and penetrative manner.

Whatever projects Duhamel undertook, he would always try, unconsciously at times, to reconcile the material world with the spiritual, the forces of destruction with those of construction, the negative with the positive. He believed fervently in the "cult of the mind," in the preservation of one's ideals, in the heart as the guiding force in life. With energy and determination, he sought to bring beauty, tolerance, humanity—and great bundles of compassion—into the world, through his literary endeavors as well as in his daily life.

"Monster-audience . . ."[1]

"**Y**OU'RE THE ONE who wrote this? Well! It's very beautiful. I'm going to produce it."[2] So spoke André Antoine, director of the famous Odéon theater in Paris, as he placed his hand resolutely on the manuscript of Duhamel's first play, *The Light (La Lumière).*

I Odéon-Antoine

To be produced by Antoine was indeed a great accomplishment. To have one's first play accepted by such a venerable man of the theater was a veritable achievement. It had been Antoine's desire to institute a special series of Saturday performances designed to encourage young dramatists in their writing careers. Each play he chose would be performed twice and, if the criticisms were favorable, then more frequently.

For a number of years Antoine had enjoyed a very special reputation with both young and old in Paris. Dismayed by the unresponsiveness of the stage to the trends of the time he had founded his own Théâtre Libre (1887–1904) and the Théâtre Antoine (1897). He had striven through the theater to bring people face to face with themselves and their environment. He had understood early that the theatrical arts must follow the patterns of reality. Actors and actresses had to talk and walk and comport themselves on stage as people did in shops, on the streets, in the subways, and in their homes, if they were to mirror life with fidelity: a smudged mirror perhaps, but recognizable all the same, offering audiences the pleasure of recognition.

What Antoine actually accomplished was the creation of a peephole theater, permitting audiences to observe a slice of life. He became the foremost sponsor of a photographic reality and almost always used real-life props in his productions. When he produced *Blanchette* by Brieux, for example, he used real accessories—a counter, a workbasket, a novel, a pipe, tobacco, and so on. On stage he built real stores, actual *bistros,* butcher shops, and neighborhood slums.[3]

Strong, vibrant in personality, Antoine had inculcated in his artists a respect and love for letters. When it came time to produce Duhamel's first play, he brought all of his knowledge and sensitivity into this venture.

The Light opened on April 8, 1911. As Duhamel wrote, in *Light on My Days,* he experienced great anxiety, as was natural certainly, on the first night when "for the first time, I found myself in the grasp of that monster-audience with its usual servants and victims, and I can certainly admit to the fact that I felt great *malaise.*"[4]

The theme of *The Light* is blindness. The heroine, Blanche, has very poor eyesight and has been sent by her family to the lake region, where the play is situated, to strengthen it. She meets Bernard, blind from birth. They fall in love. Psychological problems arise because Bernard feels inferior to her, since she has vision. One day Bernard encourages Blanche to describe the beauties of nature so that he can see them through her eyes. In so doing, she looks too continuously at the sun's rays. As a result she suffers momentary blindness and must wear a bandage over her eyes for one week. One afternoon Bernard and Blanche are walking in the woods and a terrible storm bursts. Blanche, very frightened, huddles close to Bernard. They walk rapidly through the woods and after some time realize they are lost. Blanche is desperate. She removes her bandages in order to orient herself. Just at that moment, lightning flashes through the skies and blinds her. Finally, friends locate them. They are brought back to the house. Both are blind now, and the barrier which had separated the young lovers has now been removed. Blanche and Bernard are going to marry.

Duhamel had always been interested in blindness. Perhaps his sympathies for the blind were aroused because of his own myopia. Later in life, he even became editor of a magazine devoted to Braille. There is no question but that his medical knowledge served him well in this drama. His familiarity with the psychology of the sightless, his understanding of the inner strength residing in certain types afflicted with such a loss, his compassion for the suffering and the problems of the handicapped make the protagonists in this drama poignantly and strikingly real.

Bernard, we discover during the course of the play, is blind only physically. Emotionally and spiritually, he sees more clearly and more directly into the heart and minds of human beings and situations than do those who have sight. His understanding of life is completely intuitive, perceptive, and certainly not based upon the superficial kind of sight which evaluates everything in terms of exteriors: color and form. To keep repeating the same inanities day in and day out—that "the door is brown, the grass is green"—is an indication of one's mechanical and peripheral manner of existing. Bernard resents his father's continuous attempts to ask doctors to come and examine him, in order to find some way of restoring his eyesight. Because Bernard sees even more deeply into life than Blanche, for example, who has vision, he realizes that his attraction to her is based on the beauty of her soul. He responds to her kindness as well as to the palpable descriptions she gives to him of natural forces. When she describes the brilliance of the forest, the glaze-blue of the water, the fire-red of the sun, he sees *within* these entities and reacts to their cosmic import. When Blanche does go blind, he knows that communication between them will be complete. They will be united in a world of inner brilliance where the "real eye," that which one refers to as the "Platonic eye," will forever radiate. Each will now experience life in its totality. What the world considers an infirmity, the blind protagonists look upon as even greater perfection.

Though *The Light* can be considered a "thesis play," it is far more than a drama treating a social ill. It is the work of a young poet who has sought to envelop the entire world in his grasp, an idealist whose feelings for humanity are already well developed, whose knowledge of love is very real. Moreover, the nature descriptions in this drama are replete with a lyrical quality, enhancing in this manner its visual and sonorous elements. It is through nature, certainly, that the protagonists communicate with each other on a profound and eternal level early in their relationship. They experience the pleasure and excitement aroused by nature, mirroring Duhamel's own feelings in this domain. Like Claudel who influenced Duhamel, he tries to reach the source of creation, to touch it both physically and spiritually. Trees, flowers, water strengthen him, make him want to live life fully. Mention must also be made of the finesse with which Duhamel describes the birth and growth of love. The tenderness implicit in the dialogue between Blanche and Bernard could only have been written by one who had experienced these same feelings most profoundly.

Directly after the opening Duhamel, his wife Blanche Albane, who had portrayed the play's heroine, and some friends went home to celebrate the event. That same evening Duhamel received a *pneumatique* from Antoine. It stated that he greatly admired *The Light,* but some friends with whom he had spoken after the performance had suggested shortening and tightening some passages. He also suggested that Duhamel delete part of one act which was, scenically speaking, too long. Not yet master of his art, Duhamel was unable to comply with such a request. He was incapable of rewriting a part of his play in a day or two. *The Light,* therefore, was performed on succeeding evenings—four times—as it had been on opening night, without changes.

The reviews, disparate on the whole, were encouraging enough to warrant enthusiasm on the author's part. Paul Souday felt that *The Light* "was not a happy play but that it was a good one." Gabriel Boissy in *Excelsior* declared it to be a moving drama, an original and youthful work. Régis Gignoux announced unequivocally that it marked "the arrival of a first-class author to the stage."[5]

Duhamel was encouraged by the criticisms. He began working on his second play shortly thereafter. *In the Shadow of Statues (Dans l'ombre des statues)* opened on October 26, 1912, at the Odéon.

Duhamel again treats a social problem: the psychological difficulties arising when a great man's son lives an unauthentic existence. Robert, the son of a well-known scholar, had always lived a shadowlike life. Never treated as an individual, he is unable to act on his own. He has never acquired independence of spirit and is considered by others as a duplicate, or a reflection, of his father's vibrant personality. He has been incorporated, so to speak, into his father's image to such an extent that he resembles him physically. As he matures Robert rebels inwardly against such a state of affairs, but never overtly. He does, on several occasions, however, express his dissatisfaction over the existing relationship with his fiancée Alice. The situation reaches a climax when a statue of his father is to be inaugurated, and Robert is called upon to speak at the ceremony. At this point Duhamel introduces Robert's entourage to his audience: a group of self-centered and insidious individuals, pedants, hypocrites, greedy beings who never for one moment consider the dead man and his contributions to the world of any great value, but bask in the reflected glory he brought to his town and to those who knew him. The musician, for example, who composes a cantata for the occasion, can think of the ceremony only in terms of himself and certainly never gives a thought to the dead man; likewise for the poet who writes a poem. Robert, at this point, feels that the mask he has been wearing his entire life has become intolerable. Suddenly, through an ironical turn of events he learns that he is really not the dead man's son, but the illegitimate offspring of an artist. He is overjoyed at the thought. He no longer feels imprisoned by the "image" which had always been flaunted over him. Those surrounding him misinterpret his sense of release and relief and believe that his reaction is one of consternation. They try to console him for his loss of prestige. Even Alice looks at him a bit differently now that she knows the truth. She prefers to consider him as the famous man's son, rather than the young individual he really is. His mother, unable to face the truth of the situation, begs him to continue wearing the mask and keep the secret of his real identity. At the finale, Robert falls on his knees and agrees to play out the role he has lived for all these years.

Antoine considered *In the Shadow of Statues* "magnificent."[6] Henri Bidou, writing in *Les Débats,* agreed with him: "in that the play is extremely remarkable, one sees some very beautiful scenes." He also commented on Duhamel's firm and energetic style.[7] Most of the critics, however, as well as the several audiences who witnessed the drama, did not agree with either Antoine's or Bidou's comments. They could not accept what they considered a contrived ending, the fact that Robert refused to live out his own life as it would have been normal for him to do. Robert should have left his mother and struck out on his own. Moreover, he should have fought to discover his own identity, for only in this way could he have grown and matured. Critics and audiences alike also felt that the secondary characters were far too numerous and not well incised. They detracted from the important episodes as well as from the main protagonists.

Duhamel's acidulous satire, his mordant pen, his assessment of the bourgeois, their pettiness and superficiality, struck deeply. More important, perhaps, was the fact that his play was the outgrowth of personal experience. As a youth he had been forced to live under the dominion of an irascible, highly impulsive, quixotic father. Unlike Robert, the hero of his drama, Duhamel shed the autocratic atmosphere of his home. When he acted decisively and independently, he was imbued with a sense of relief. Only at this point was he able to grow as an individual.

Duhamel was quite disheartened by the reception *In the Shadow of Statues* received. He felt that Antoine was partially to blame because of a frightful tactical error he had made. On the very day of the play's opening Antoine had published an article in which he claimed Duhamel's play to be a veritable masterpiece. Psychologically speaking, it proved to be a disastrous move. Audiences are annoyed rather than seduced by such brash pronouncements. Parisian critics were undoubtedly alienated. Léon Blum, for example, one of the most prominent critics of the time, wrote that M. Duhamel might certainly write masterpieces one day, "but this event had not yet taken place."[8]

Duhamel's plays were certainly not on a par with the other dramatists Antoine had produced in his theater: Hauptmann, Ibsen, Tolstoy, and the like; nor did his work have the acerbity or the force of the Naturalist writers such as Courteline, Becque, or Renard. Yet there was something fresh and spontaneous, an urgency and a lyrical quality which was Duhamel's and which needed developing.

II *Théâtre des Arts-Rouché*

Duhamel was not one to remain despondent for any length of time. He was a young man of action and vigor. He was determined to write more plays and perhaps turn to another theatrical director for future works. When he learned of Jacques Rouché's new theatrical endeavor, the Théâtre des Arts, which he had founded in 1911, Duhamel went to see him. Actually he was answering the director's call for new authors, new plays. He submitted a five-act drama *The Combat (Le Combat)* to Rouché and it was accepted.

Rouché was an extraordinary person in his own right. Influenced by the writings of Edward Gordon Craig and Adolphe Appia, Jacques Rouché published a very important work *Modern Theatrical Art* (1910) in which he outlined his ideas concerning directing, staging, lighting, costuming, decor, everything relating to play production. It could be said that Rouché "felt" the theater, that he "understood" it and that his theories were never static, but responded always to the individual works he produced.[9]

Rouché's malleable theatrical concepts were revolutionary for the time. His small Théâtre des Arts, situated on the Boulevard des Batignolles, had already attracted many artists and writers to his fold. He had won a fine reputation for exciting productions such as *The Brothers Karamazov,* adapted by Jacques Copeau and Croué. These productions included such names, later to become famous, as Louis Jouvet and Charles Dullin. The atmosphere pervading the Théâtre des Arts was almost monkish in its sense of dedication.

The Combat opened on March 14, 1913, and featured Blanche Albane in the female lead. Like the other Duhamel works, this latest theatrical endeavor also had a thesis: the visionary does not always reap the benefits of his ideas, rather those who survive the ordeal, the strong, inevitably do.

The drama takes place in a region in France which has been ravaged by constant inundations. A feudal family, including a grandfather aged ninety, a son aged sixty and a grandson aged twenty-five who suffers from tuberculosis, are the patriarchs of this region. Gérard, the youngest of the family, is inspired to help his countrymen; he has a feeling for others, instead of constantly dwelling upon his own welfare. His father and grandfather, however, are obsessed with their own health, their aches and pains, their financial situation and the like. Though Gérard is physically ill, he conceives of a plan to build a dike, encourages the peasants to break ground, to see beyond their petty and vicious ways, to work for the sake of the community. He infuses a sense of optimism into what, until this time, has been a "dead" village. The dike is finally built, just in time, because another flood is about to sweep over the land. Gérard, however, is dying at this point and though it was he who inspired the edifice, Michael, his cousin, the physically strong, reaps the laurels for having been instrumental in carrying out the plans. Gérard's fiancée, Marie, hails Michael, as do the rest of the townspeople. Gérard dies alone and forgotten, imbued, nonetheless, with the great satisfaction of having helped humanity.

The Combat, though written in verse, which gives this play a rather stilted effect at times, has some masterful strokes in it. The earthiness of the dialogue, for example, forces a certain kind of peasant atmosphere. One can actually feel the succulent language, the innuendos, the turbulence of their thoughts, the despair in some of their imagistic expressions. The description of the land, its dampness, the water encroaching ever more deeply upon the fertile areas, drowning all with its merciless march, is interwoven into the plot with dexterity. Indeed, the entire play revolves around the symbol of the river which inundates not only the land but the very air the characters breathe.

The scenes of the peasants laboring to break ground, trying slowly and arduously to build a dike, are worthy of a Zola or of a Maupassant. Not only is the dialogue itself effective and strong, but the peasants' cant—their philosophy of life embedded in selfishness, laziness, and a very special brand of greed which is part and parcel of the French peasant personality—comes through in this play every step of the way, and with gusto. Visually speaking, the peasant scenes are reminiscent of

Breughel and Millet paintings. The striking hues Duhamel has injected into his verbal descriptions, the way they are projected on stage, the placement of all the characters in a variety of groupings, filling the empty performing areas, are all exciting.

Another important factor which cannot be overlooked in *The Combat* is the attention paid to medical problems. In this period Duhamel was still working full time in a laboratory and writing only in his spare hours. For this reason he still centered his thoughts around what he knew best. The true-to-life allusions to Gérard's tuberculosis, to the painful rheumatism suffered by the older people, lend an authentic and credible tone to the entire piece.

There are, however, certain technical inadequacies which must be noted in *The Combat*. These stem from the fact that Duhamel tries to increase the suspense by having Gérard faint, by attempting to hide his condition from the peasants, by putting up a bold front. These devices are artificial and, therefore, detract from the play's Naturalistic and somber tone.

III *Théâtre du Vieux-Colombier-Copeau*

Though *Combat* was performed twenty times, Duhamel, on this occasion, was not satisfied with his work. He felt that it lacked true inspiration. Moreover, he decided that the Théâtre des Arts was not stimulating him sufficiently. He needed a different kind of theatrical enterprise, he felt, which would be more imaginative, more personal, and simpler in its goals. When Jacques Copeau announced his intention of leaving the Théâtre des Arts and founding his own Théâtre du Vieux-Colombier, Duhamel became truly enthusiastic over this venture. He felt that this new theatrical enterprise would answer not only his purposes but those of his actress wife.

Jacques Copeau was intent upon ridding the theater of all commercialism, inertia, ignorance, disorder, and lack of discipline. He wanted to reconstruct theatrical art from the base up. His was an expression of pure fanaticism in the world of the theater. His new theater was to be designed along simple and classical lines. He rejected the boulevard theaters with their heavy ornamentation, the gold plate, the rococo. He sought fresh techniques for achieving more powerful and suggestive visual and dramatic effects, while strictly adhering to the import of the text. He would also try to make finished and versatile actors out of unleavened human talent.

While the Théâtre du Vieux-Colombier was being renovated in June,

1913, Copeau took his newly formed troupe which included Louis Jouvet, Charles Dullin, and Blanche Albane among others, to the Limon in the region of La Ferté-sous-Jouarre, about an hour away from Paris by train. On arrival in the lovely green countryside, his actors were boarded at the homes of nearby farmers and spent the summer there rehearsing out-of-doors every day, sometimes five hours without interruption. Copeau made every demand upon his actors. They swam, fenced, and danced; their bodies became supple and strong.[10]

Duhamel and his wife spent most of their summer with the Vieux-Colombier company at the Limon. He did not find commuting to Paris daily or his work at the laboratory overtaxing. His enthusiasm overcame whatever lassitude might have set in. Whenever he could, he watched the troupe rehearsing, learning the techniques of the acting craft from the bottom up. It was at this period that he began writing his first comedy, *The Work of Athletes (L'Oeuvre des athlètes)*, a humorous and satiric drama in which he takes a Tartuffe-like character to task. This play, however, would not be performed until April 10, 1920. A series of horrendous events were to intrude during the intervening years.

In 1914, at the beginning of World War I, Georges Duhamel volunteered to serve in a mobile ambulance unit. For four painful and traumatic years death surrounded him on every side. Acting with extreme courage and humanity, he did his best to help the lot of the wounded soldier. One day, his chief, Dr. Antonin Gosset, asked him to write a little comedy to entertain the wounded recuperating in the hospital.

Duhamel complied and wrote *Lapointe et Ropiteau*, a short play based on an actual incident which has taken place in 1916 on the Somme, when Duhamel was busy in the ambulance tent caring for the wounded. At that time he had overheard a conversation between two wounded men who were comparing their ailments, each considering his own far worse than those of his companion.

Duhamel's purpose in writing this one-act play was of course to console the war victims and to amuse them as well. He did not want to arouse tears but rather to alleviate sorrow. He realized in this connection that "one can amuse men by painting their own miseries before them." The play, which features two soldiers, ripples with wit and satire. It consists of a dialogue between Lapointe, whose left arm is set in a complicated apparatus, and Ropiteau, who is on crutches.

Lapointe and Ropiteau was performed twenty times in ambulances, outdoors, before men lying on stretchers and sitting or standing. In his preface to the play Duhamel declares that the memory of these performances will remain indelibly fixed in his mind forever. He could hardly believe that he had extracted laughter from men whose plight was so agonizing, whose futures were so precarious. Yet, he had succeeded. They laughed during the entire half hour, which was the length of the play. As for the author, he added: "Never has laughter been so close to wrenching tears from me."

When the war ended and Duhamel returned to civilian life he waited two more years before Jacques Copeau and the Vieux-Colombier produced his character comedy *The Work of Athletes*. In this drama Duhamel wanted to give the impression of universality, implying that the story he was about to relate could take place anywhere at any time. The drama revolves around a principal character Beloeuf whom Duhamel portrays as an uninspired writer, the editor of the magazine *The Work of Spiritual Athletes,* a man who pretends to have inventive gifts and formulates astounding and fantastic systems which he tries to impose upon others by using big words and speaking in sonorous tones. Duhamel introduces this pompous man into a normal household, that of a druggist, Auboyer. As the action proceeds, the druggist's daughters fall in love with Beloeuf, indicating how contagious is the silliness of overadmiration and to what extent it can influence a naive family. A Tartuffe situation is recreated here with Denis, the son, the only member of the family to remain impervious to the wiles of the parasite.

Duhamel was certainly influenced by Molière. Some scenes in *The Work of Athletes* are reminiscent of episodes in *Monsieur de Pourceaugnac, Tartuffe,* and *Les Femmes savantes.* The entire mood of irony, acerbity, and humor can also be traced to the seventeenth-century master of comedy, even the depiction of the puppetlike secondary characters who are like trees bending in the wind whenever Beloeuf enters and pronounces his ratiocinations. Certain critics were annoyed by Duhamel's poor "imitation," as they expressed it, of Molière's genius. Such an influence, however, was not denied by Duhamel. On the contrary, Molière was his inspiration and he had written the play with this in mind.

The critics as a whole were not enthusiastic over this "comedy of mores," this "character comedy," because they felt the plot to be scant, the development to be uninteresting, the situation rather trivial. Henry Bordeaux, however, was convinced that the satire of the ambitious hypocrite was quite remarkable and that *The Work of*

Athletes "was one of the most vigorously comic works, the healthiest and most colorful that he had seen in a long while."

IV *The Pitoëff Company*

Duhamel, sensitive as are most artists, smarted under the blows of the caustic remarks leveled his way. He did not, therefore, pursue his dramatic undertakings with the Vieux-Colombier company, but a year later, he turned to another extraordinary acting group, Georges and Ludmilla Pitoëff.

The Pitoëffs, born in Tiflis, Russia, had founded their own acting company in Switzerland in 1918. Georges Pitoëff was an astonishing director; sensitive, a visionary, an idealist, he despised everything which smacked of routine and bathed all he produced in a half-lit world of mystery. He was a master at sounding out depths, of forcing out the soul of a work, of bringing out the characters. As Duhamel himself said: "What a profound love for the scenic sacrament!"[1][2]

The Pitoëffs performed Duhamel's one-act comedy *When you Wish (Quand vous voudrez)* in Geneva, on February 5, 1921. In this work, as light and as accelerated in pace as a Marivaux comedy, Duhamel satirizes small talk, superficial quarrels and the pettiness of two couples who seek to buy a country place. The moral of this tingling bit of irony which is the play, is to strike while the iron is hot; otherwise opportunity vanishes.

Two years later, on October 24, 1923, the Pitoëffs, now ensconced in the Studio des Champs-Elysées theater in Paris, performed Duhamel's *The Day of Avowals (La Journée des aveux).* This drama relates the story of a pseudoscholar who has decided to give his money to a family whom he considers happy and living in harmony. He visits the Foulon family, prepared to make his bequest. He discovers much to his shock that what he has thought of as "ideal" is in fact sordid. The father is unfaithful; the thirty-five-year-old daughter is an unfortunate and bigoted old maid; the younger girl is a flirt who wants to run away from home. The mother is a saintly creature, endures the pain. At the play's end, however, the situation is adjusted: the husband returns to his wife, the daughters find happiness in their own way.

Despite the fact that *The Day of Avowals* is a rather mediocre comedy and was considered as such by the critics, there are, nevertheless, very humorous incidents, conversations, and characterizations. The role of the General, for example, portrayed by Louis Jouvet, was a masterpiece in conception. Though it was a minor part, Jouvet studied every word and phrase, every gesture, to such an extent that he won laurels. The critics commented on the profundity and precision he injected into his part and the utterly ridiculous impression he made each time he stepped onstage. Humorous incidents take place onstage in scenes between Heglin, the scholar who seeks to make the bequest, and Madame Foulon. She, who had always wanted to sniff snuff and who had been forbidden from doing so by her husband because he is convinced it lacks decorum, indulges together with her guest in this mutual vice. The scene is *droll* because of the dichotomy between what she considers to be a crime and the innocuous nature of her act.

What is most interesting in this drama is that Duhamel created double personalities: beings who are forever giving the impression of knowing calm and a reasonable amount of joy, but whose other aspects come through only after their masks have been removed, revealing characters which are distraught, anguished, and deeply sorrowful. The stifled feelings and passions, their desire to express their love and tenderness for others are constantly frustrated, not only because of social conventions but because of man's frequent desire to "hurt," his oblivious attitude toward the welfare of others. Happiness, in the last analysis, exists only when people "hide," at least partially, their desires, in an attempt to spare the feelings of others. Happiness is something which can exist at certain periods, a state one must struggle to achieve. The Foulon family does not differ from any other social unit. As Sophie, one of the daughters declares, "This unfortunate house is similar in all respects to any other." It is through love alone, through a sensitive and kind approach to all members of the family, that one can achieve harmony and happiness.

The Day of Avowals was Duhamel's last play. Many conjectures have been offered for this turn of events. The most acceptable, certainly, is the discouragement he experienced at the hands of the critics. Indeed, Duhamel himself had written several times that a dramatist's work is a "calvary," a "torture," that each time a play is produced it must confront a group of critics filled with preconceived ideas and grudges, audiences who cough, whose chairs squeak, who move about in their seats throughout the performance.[13]

Although Duhamel cannot be considered a great playwright, his irony and his bent for satire are certainly well developed and interesting. His plays usually follow a pattern and have a thesis: frequently they are endowed with a main character around which a series of secondary characters constellate, usually mirroring or disagreeing with the protagonist's intent. Most frequently the main character suffers from extreme solitude and is unable to break through the barriers which seem to stifle his *élan,* except through love. Love seems to be the one way of surfacing. Influences are also detected in Duhamel's plays: the realism of Ibsen is discernible in *The Combat,* the humor and wit of Molière in *The Day of Avowals,* the lyrical quality of a Claudel in *The Light.*

Duhamel also contributed certain essays on theatrical subjects: *The Auspasian Letters (Lettres d'Auspasie)* in which several essays are devoted to his conception of the dramatic arts and are entitled "On Orators" ("Sur les orateurs"), and "On the Theater" ("Sur le théâtre") (1922); also *Essay on a Dramatic Renaissance (Essai sur une renaissance dramatique)* (1926). In these works Duhamel speaks forcefully against a didactic theater as well as against the stress laid upon decor, costumes. The most important element in the theater is the dramatist's text. Duhamel reserves some spleen for the triple travesty which each dramatist must endure. When the creative writer composes his work in the privacy of his room he conceives of his drama in one way. When it is operated upon by directors, actors, decorators, costume designers, and those who share in creating the final spectacle, the dichotomy between what the artist had originally conceived and the finished product is frequently heartbreaking. What remains is a caricature, a puppet show. If the dramatist feels that his troubles are over after he has seen the final dress rehearsals, he is mistaken. The worst is yet to come. The audience, sitting pat in their seats, enjoying or criticizing what they are seeing, has the final word. Still more painful is the reception given to the play by the critics.

Though the theater may be a brilliant and glorious field for some creative people, it was rejected by Duhamel in favor of the novel and essay form which are, in the last analysis, "a debate between two minds." As Duhamel adds: "It is in solitude that the book awaits the reader. Savory hour, intimate colloquy, confrontation of two people outside of space and time. . . . It is not a gift alone, it is an exchange."[14] It would be the novel then.

CHAPTER 3

"You Hear! You Hear! It's War!"[1]

N O SOONER HAD hostilities broken out in 1914 than Duhamel volunteered as an army doctor. He served for fifty-one months, he tells us in his biography, in a mobile surgical unit not far from the front. In his four years of service, he performed two thousand operations and cared for four thousand wounded.

The ghastly sights Duhamel saw about him, coupled with the constant toil required of a surgeon, had a traumatic effect upon this sensitive young man. He was seeing life for the first time, in its most painful, primitive, brutal, and yet most courageous aspects. Faced with dying in all stages and forms, Duhamel empathetically experienced the fears and anguishes of those who were drawing their last breaths, of those who would return to civilian life maimed and abnormal, Duhamel did not react to the spectacle negatively; this holocaust taught him the meaning of life—that most precious gift given to man—and how it could be experienced most effectively.

During the early stages of the war Duhamel worked under the most trying conditions. He operated much of the time within fire range, without proper equipment, minus those facilities used to alleviate the pain of the wounded. He lived, breathed, and slept with the stench of gangrene and mutilated flesh about him; he heard exploding shells bursting with their macabre rhythms; he felt congealed with the cold, clammy from the dampness of the rain which frequently fell down in sheets in the heat of summer and poured in torrents in the cold months; his heart was torn by the groans of crying men. Duhamel lived the suffering of these human beings who either survived their ordeal or passed away still fighting fate.

Duhamel needed an outlet, some means of expressing his shock and revulsion at the horrors he was facing daily. Release, however, from the emotional pain he endured was not all he needed. He was no egocentric. Rather, he was moved by his enormous capacity for compassion, his feelings for humanity. He wanted to inform society of the extreme heroism of his men, the pain they endured without whimpering, the lives they would have to face if they survived and were compelled, thereby, to face their friends and families. He wanted society to begin to work for these soldiers, to think in terms of rehabilitating them when they returned without an arm or arms, without legs, without eyes. Moreover, he was determined to inform those who knew nothing of the terrors of wars and so spoke in vacuous concepts, those armchair philosophers who sat back in their heated and comfortable rooms, deciding the fate of the world and the destiny of its youth from afar. He wanted these people, oblivious to the realities of the situation, to feel repugnance for this horrendous evil which had permeated the world, this onslaught of barbarity, this unleashing of man's most insidious instincts. Duhamel did not want those who had experienced the slaughter to forget it, nor those who had known nothing about it, the children, the next generation. Duhamel, who knew people well, was aware of the fact that people do forget misery with alacrity, that suffering is frequently met with harshness and callousness; that compassion is a rare quality. Duhamel had a message for humanity in his two war books: *The New Book of Martyrs (Vie des martyrs)* and *Civilization (Civilisation)*.

I The New Book of Martyrs

There is no dearth of historical works in which battles are described with precision and depth. Vigny, Stendhal, Mérimée, Tolstoi, Dorgelès, Kessel and so many more were masters in this domain. Novels, narratives, sketches, and vignettes have always been potent factors in acquainting society with the horrors involved in the outbreak and clash of hate. Rare is the work, however, written at the time the actual turmoil is being experienced. Duhamel wrote *The New Book of Martyrs* during those years when battles were raging about him. There is, therefore, an earthy and authentic quality which permeates the work, the power and energy which emanates from a human being who is actually witnessing momentous events.

Duhamel wrote *The New Book of Martyrs* at night or in spare moments. It was at these times that he jotted down, on bits of note paper he found lying about, his ideas, impressions of the work, and the functions he performed daily. He then recopied these vignettes, giving them some order and form, after which he sent them to his wife who would in turn copy them by hand. It was she who presented them to their friend Alfred Vallette, editor of the *Mercure de France.* They were published in 1917 under the title *Vie des martyrs (The New Book of Martyrs).*

The New Book of Martyrs consists of nine sketches in which Duhamel describes the army experiences he lived through with the realism and incisiveness of a master. It was not merely the outside event or situation which he set down on paper; he also succeeded in capturing the souls of those men who live on eternally in his book.

Beneath their bandages, there are wounds you can't even imagine. At the wound's depths within the mutilation itself, there is an extraordinary soul which becomes agitated and exalted, furtive, which doesn't manifest itself easily, which expresses itself with candor, and which I would so like to have you understand.[2]

The New Book of Martyrs is a "sojourn in suffering," a true experience in martyrdom as lived by twentieth-century protagonists, a volume in which Duhamel sketches his impressions of and reactions to living situations: the soldiers brought to him on stretchers or dragged or carried into the mobile ambulance unit and the makeshift hospitals to be operated upon. It recounts the stories of all types of wounded soldiers: one who has just awakened from anesthesia to discover that his hands are merely a "souvenir," or another who searches tremulously to find the end of his body, only to learn with anguish that both of his legs have been cut off.[3] *The New Book of Martyrs* relates in poignant terms the fear and agony which overwhelm the man confronted with the loss of a limb, the tears which trickle from his eyes as the full impact of his condition is revealed to him, the pain he tries to bury as he turns his head away from the stare of onlookers; descriptions of the soldier who coughs ceaselessly because a bullet has been lodged closely to his lung, who spits up with pain written in his eyes and who struggles for the next breath to keep life going; or the young lad whose suffering is too great to bear and whose will to live, therefore, diminishes and is finally extinguished.

The New Book of Martyrs comprises still other vignettes. Duhamel depicts the soldier whose agony is so great that it forces black sweat to flow freely over his ashen face, the contrast lending terror to the entire picture. "Man is no longer frightened, at this moment," writes Duhamel, "but the flesh remains fearful."[4] Clinical details are not spared: the crescendo of emotions as they overwhelm a victim after an operation when the anesthetic wears off or when no anesthetic is available, the eruption of grief as it incises itself into the features of the men who have sacrificed what they sought most to keep—their lives.

On certain days the wounded come to the tents en masse, Duhamel writes, litters and stretchers waiting like cars on an automobile assembly line. Frequently the doctors and aides do not even have time to undress the sick, to clean them properly before putting them on the operating table. The mud, therefore, clings to their clothes, encrusts itself onto their bodies while vermin and lice crawl about the sores and then permeate the bandages. All of this takes place while small and large rats run in and out of the tents. It is no wonder there were outbreaks of meningitis and dysentery and that Duhamel himself suffered most persistently from terrible sore throats, high fevers, and moments when his throat became so contracted that he could not breathe and choked to the point of becoming unconscious.

Duhamel's reportage is not merely that of a physician acquainting his readers with the clinical details of the cases he handled, nor is it a compendium of sketches in the style of a Balzac, a Zola, or a Goncourt. A man with a mission, Duhamel recounts with compassion the calvary of the sick as they arrive at his makeshift hospital, until their death or their release from it. The stoicism revealed by these men when confronted with pain and death, the emotional ordeal they have to experience, the moral trial of learning the bitter fact that they are no longer masters of their bodies, was a lesson in control and an extraordinary understanding of self. With extreme empathy, never maudlin, however, Duhamel describes the fears and philosophies of the men under his scrutiny, the words they speak, which seem to emerge from the inner man, their desire to adjust and to return to the world to which they have given so much and for which in return they will be shunned, considered abnormal—pariahs of sorts.

Though the subject matter is serious, Duhamel's narrative is not macabre. While describing the human condition, he inserts humorous anecdotes, witty and satiric statements which alleviate the progressively somber notes. His personal style is never burdened with glowing treatises or with attempts at artistic effects. Rather, he contents himself with simple, energetic, straightforward sentences into which he injects some dialogue here and there, altering, thereby, the rhythm, creating variety and increased interest.

II Civilization

Duhamel's second volume devoted to his war experience, *Civilization 1914–17,* was published under the pseudonym of Denis Thévenin. He chose anonymity because he did not want his personality to intrude upon the incidents he was relating. Let the facts speak for themselves, he reasoned. Nor did he want his work to be considered as "literature," strictly speaking, or evaluated in those terms. Rather, he suggested that *Civilization* be looked upon as a social document to which society would pay attention, enabling it to understand the breach which would exist between the soldier returning from the front (especially if he were wounded or maimed) and the civilian who had not the faintest notion of the meaning of human suffering.

In the sixteen sketches which constitute *Civilization,* Duhamel relates the plight of some of the men he knew during the war period, their psychological and emotional reactions to suffering, their heroism and optimism in the face of battle and death. In addition to these descriptions, with which the book is replete, there emerges from these pages a growing sense of anger each time the doctor fails to restore life. As a medical man, Duhamel was struck by the degradation which overwhelmed him each time feelings of powerlessness intruded upon his life, as they did during those moments when he could not prevent death, when he viewed mass slaughter on the battlefields, constant killing, trench warfare, disease. Anything that impairs life, he declares, is an unmitigated insult to the doctor.

There are several stories which stand out indelibly in the mind of the reader—one, in particular, concerning Lieutenant Dauche who has received shrapnel in his head. Certain bits which have lodged in his brain cannot be removed. Death is inevitable. Though the narrator knows that Lieutenant Dauche's death is going to result, he wants to spare the soldier this knowledge, since Dauche is convinced that he is going to recover, slowly but surely. As time wanders on the narrator, who is himself recuperating from a shoulder wound, grows increasingly apprehensive. He begins to suffer desperately and empathetically for his friend. Indeed, the knowledge that Lieutenant Danche must die gnaws at him mercilessly, to the extent that it drains him of all of his strength, saps his vitality, and he can do nothing but remain in bed. The anguish felt by the narrator becomes that much more incisive when contrasted with Dauche's optimism, as he keeps planning for the future. The greater the gap between the men, the more gruesome grows the relationship. "The idea that this man was going to die shed itself upon all of my thoughts, to the point of extracting from me all stability, all courage, all ability to act."[5] When the narrator finally feels strength returning to his limb, he realizes that he must hide his feelings of sadness, that he must accept his friend's demise as part of the routine of life. He is shocked, nevertheless, with the realization that he is, unconsciously, wishing for the Lieutenant's speedy death, because he can no longer bear to watch him grow increasingly weak. One day, as they are strolling together in the fields, the Lieutenant falls down, unconscious. The narrator then musters all of his strength, carries his friend back to the hospital, and there, "I let death labor and I waited until it had ended its work."[6] Only when death has clasped his friend in its embrace can the narrator weep.

In another sketch Duhamel describes the courage expended by a wounded youth whose leg has just been amputated. The joint had been so severely shattered by bursting shell fire that the stump itself keeps bleeding. Each time the soldier is sent to the infirmary in haste to prevent more of life's fluid from withdrawing, the doctors in charge think the leg will mend. Hemorrhaging nevertheless follows the day after. "It made one think of a fruit upon which vermin had been working," writes Duhamel.[7] One day the bleeding will stop. This thought is perhaps the doctor's only consolation.

When drawing the picture of a twenty-year-old lad suffering from meningitis, or another whose eye has been shot out, Duhamel does not intend to complain or to solicit pity from others, but rather to educate an ignorant public, to acquaint them with the plight of the man on the battlefield, to force those at home who speak so glibly in terms of war, who meditate with superficiality upon the term "civilization," to reassess their views and creations. What does the word "civilization" mean? What do the achievements of a "civilized" society imply? Destruction? Hatred? Ruin? Anger? When Duhamel contemplated the debris on a battlefield, the rows and rows of hospital beds nearby, he could feel nothing but contempt for those who had unleashed such fury and wondered what real purpose civilization served.

Certainly Duhamel was well aware of the fact that the mechanical age was here to stay, that the inventiveness of this era furnished doctors with many needed instruments designed to save lives. By the same token, the horrendous weapons and machines constructed by these same inventors to hasten destruction were anathema to him. Civilization, as far as Duhamel was concerned, does not reside in mechanical progress or improvement, but rather in the heart, in man's growing appeal to goodness, in the development of the higher faculties of consciousness.

Though Duhamel felt the agony of his men, heard the cries of pain, smelled the rot of decay and putrefied flesh, watched tenderly as life withdrew from so many, still he was not consumed with hatred for the enemy. Such feelings were foreign to him. His weapon for showing disdain was irony, ferocious satire, soliciting in this manner bitter laughter, inflicting upon the carefree and the irresponsible the pungent feelings of guilt. Realistic images, incisive portrayals, panoramic views were also effective in arousing disgust on the part of the reader, as, for example, in the following passages in which the Battle of the Marne is described:

The disorder on a battlefield, its richness in carrion, the abnormal accumulation of animals, of men, of spoiled food; for all these reasons there was a formidable blossoming of flies that year. They seemed to have made an appointment with each other from all parts of the globe, to be present at an exceptionally solemn moment. There were all types; and the human world, giving vent to its hatreds, remained defenseless against this odious invasion. During an entire summer, they were mistresses, queens, and food was not spared them.[8]

When *Civilization* was acclaimed by the French public and won for its author the much coveted Goncourt Prize, Duhamel's authorship was revealed. He felt no joy, however, at the reception of the award. He wrote *Civilization,* he had declared many times, not as entertainment, but as a reportage designed to help prevent future military action, to acquaint society with the atrocities of mass killing. Instead, his work elicited articles in praise of his style, his verbal prowess, the exactitude and finesse of his descriptions, the depth of his vision. Rather than arousing feelings of disgust and hatred for war, *Civilization* had just the effect Duhamel had hoped to avoid; it accustomed people to the horrors of war; it hardened them toward suffering.

Bitterness permeated the author's heart.

III   The Search for Grace

The spiritual effect of what Duhamel had lived through during the war years was expressed most simply and beautifully in *The Search for Grace (La Recherche de la grâce).* In this volume Duhamel writes of feelings of grace, those he himself had known so poignantly. His interpretation of grace, however, is not a dogmatic one. Duhamel was not a churchgoer and did not believe in the tenets of his religion. Indeed, when he met a priest on the battlefield and asked how he could be pardoned in order to alleviate feelings of guilt and distress at the thought of his medical impotence, the priest said merely, "Say three Paters and three Aves." Duhamel's reaction was immediate and intense. He was disgusted with the priest and labeled him "corrupt."[9]

Grace is a feeling which invades man when he is in touch with nature, Duhamel wrote, when he feels the intensity of rapport with the cosmos. If a man is struck cruelly by fate and if he succeeds in overcoming the resulting anger, accepting his lot and acting positively in terms of his disability, then he has known grace. Grace is harmony and balance; it is a means of appraising life in its entirety, abiding by the fact that man's earthly tenure is merely temporary, that he passes through it as one does when crossing from one side of the street to another. One tries to function as well as possible, to go the whole length of the trajectory, enjoying as fully as possible the scenery involved.

Perhaps Duhamel's happiest moments during the gruesome war period were during that time when his own child, Bernard, was born. The birth filled him with strength, with a desire to remake the world; it imbued him with optimism, with the thought that all would be well, that man would stop his fruitless combat, cease his merciless atrocities.

IV *Ethical Concepts*

In *Conversations During the Tumult (Entretiens dans le tumulte),* published in 1919, a year after *The Search for Grace,* Duhamel suggests that man must progress in the ethical and human domain in order to keep pace with his rapid mechanical developments. Higher values must be instituted in society, with less emphasis paid to the material aspects of existence, and more import placed upon its moral side. Duhamel also advocates the necessity of permitting the human heart to speak forth freely, to cry if need be, to breathe its sorrows and joys. The heart has a way frequently of solving seemingly impossible problems. To be avoided, however, is a callous attitude toward difficulties as well as an escapist or defeatist point of view. Insensitivity, harshness, or negativism can pave the way for another holocaust, he declares. One must never be indifferent to adversity, blind or deaf to impossible and unpleasant situations. The blood which has been shed, Duhamel had reiterated during four long years, should not be given in vain. For this reason, he repeats once again what he had said in his first two war books: the horrors of war should not be forgotten; martyrdom should be ever present in the hearts and minds of those who have not experienced war at close range. In this manner, political sophistry and armchair philosophy can be avoided.

You are going to return to your worn morality, your old and compromising religions, your condemned social and political institutions, your glass of absinthe . . . your daily shipwreck. . . . You will only set this piece of wreckage afloat again. Why did you let us believe it would be a beautiful and new caravelle, that you would cast upon the purple seas again. . . . You will not build a solid house with old stones. If but one person, at the first sign of peace, speaks of a new life, if one person speaks of a resurrection and not of beginning anew, then eternity will be a sweet thing for our exhausted souls.[10]

Neither society as Duhamel knew it, nor religion as it was practiced, could ameliorate man's inability to make peace with himself and his fellow beings. Only understanding, compassion, and the desire to forgive could perhaps dispel another worldwide conflagration. Hatred, revenge, and viciousness could lead to nothing but renewed slaughter. It was with the hope of educating his compatriots that Duhamel wrote his *Conversations During the Tumult* and other polemical works which were to come.

Despite the fact that *Conversations During the Tumult* was a sincere and reflective essay filled with reminiscences, it was marred perhaps by an oversimplification of man's plight and the possibilities of its being altered. The vigor, the freshness, the virility, and stirring emotions replete in *The New Book of Martyrs* and *Civilization* seemed to be lacking in this more cerebral and detached essay. Duhamel had not yet resolved the problem of combining philosophical probings with the art of narration.

V The Heart's Domain

The Heart's Domain (La Possession du monde) (1919) is a long essay in which Duhamel succeeds in provoking the intellectual as well as the emotional interest of his readers. In this work he is intent upon discovering, if not an answer, at least a path which might help man face his existence in a positive manner. Though the work does make frequent mention of his own turbulent war experiences, it is actually a hymn to life and to happiness. It could be said that had Duhamel not been exposed to the horrors of death and of agony in its myriad forms and phases during World War I, he might not have been so intent upon living life fully and having his compatriots appreciate the meaning of existence.

The Heart's Domain was begun in 1917, during the bleak days preceding the armistice, when Duhamel was still operating around the clock, when his features were marked with exhaustion. It was completed in 1918. It is an essay which reveals the wisdom and depth of a man who has successfully passed from youth to maturity. *The Heart's Domain* could certainly have been a depressing and despairing study of the human condition, a diatribe against blood and gore. It is none of these things. It is rather a positive work in which the author has made a concerted effort to seize from his experiences all those elements which could be useful to man in general, and in so doing to formulate a credo. *The Heart's Domain* is an analytical assessment of man's plight in a modern mechanized world of steel and granite.

The Heart's Domain, Duhamel wrote in his preface, emerged from the meditations resulting from his own deep sense of solitude. Solitude must be understood in the philosophical sense. It does not imply isolation. On the contrary, Duhamel was always surrounded by people: by the sick and the dying, by work and turmoil. Exhausted and unnerved from the prolonged physical and emotional strain he was undergoing, he withdrew into his own inner domain at certain moments in the day. He isolated himself emotionally from those who engulfed him and in so doing found the capacity to delve within himself. Solitude then became productive, a learning device.

In *The Heart's Domain* Duhamel is in search of values which could better man's lot on earth. He does not, however, have recourse to organized religion, as he had so clearly stated in *The Search for Grace,* but to something far freer and, in terms of himself, far more profound. Duhamel feels that the church works hand in hand with governments, that it is no longer a spiritual force, nor can it succor anyone today. In fact, he recounts several highly unsatisfactory conversations with priests which seemed to bring to an end any hope he might have had in working with the church or its ministers. Indeed, Duhamel stated throughout the war years and afterward as well, and most forcefully, that he had nothing in common with the clergy, these so-called men of God, that faith had been reduced by them to a series of mechanical devices.

In *The Heart's Domain* Duhamel declares most emphatically that "happiness is the goal of life," for the individual as well as for humanity in general. Unfortunately, people are for the most part so immersed in their own worlds, their work, their particular grief or joy, that they are unable to see beyond their present turmoil into the future. Their lives, therefore, seem to lack vision and frequently purpose. They are incapable of experiencing the inner joy which comes with a sense of awareness of the simple beauties surrounding individuals in their daily existence. Happiness, as understood by Duhamel, does not imply voluptuousness or hedonistic pleasures; these are of a fleeting nature. His brand of "happiness" is measured in depth and implies a capacity to penetrate the very core of life, its substance, and to draw from it all that is meaningful to each individual. Such an attitude can bring about feelings of self-fulfillment. As the title indicates, happiness results from "the possession of the world," the knowledge and rapture encountered when witnessing life: breathing, moving about, walking in a field, watching a blade of grass shift in the wind, looking at a cluster of violets, inhaling the subtle aroma emanating from this living entity, viewing its color and form, experiencing the joy of completeness and perfection offered by this small object. Though the blade of grass and the cluster of violets may not have any material value and certainly could not possibly be appreciated by the avid or the greedy, the enjoyment of the exquisite beauty and the miracle of its existence should fill the onlooker's heart with immeasurable joy.

When Duhamel speaks of happiness he does not envisage an ideal or unreasonable state—paradise. Happiness is within the reach of everyone, he implies. It requires a desire for discovery, a search within, a gentleness and sensitivity to all facets of life and an open mind. To discover life requires a *soul*.[11]

The soul to which Duhamel alludes so frequently in this opus is not to be associated with any kind of formal, religious, credolike concoction, but rather can be compared to a vague kind of sensation, a spiritual inclination or feeling which invades the entire being and permits the discovery of a bond existing between the earth and the self. Once this sensation has come into consciousness, the gap which exists between the individual and his fellow beings can be bridged. At this juncture, one may experience harmony and balance within one's frame of reference. The soul can now become manifest. Each thinking and feeling individual has the capacity to discover his soul, to cultivate it and the world it reflects.[12] The ability to peer within and without, to become conscious of matter and spirit can be known through a protracted sounding out of self. When such feelings and notions have been realized, they must be forever renewed and reworked, because nothing in the cosmos is static. Happiness and harmony—even the discovery of the soul—are like water, flowing and shifting ceaselessly, constantly on the verge of drying up or of wasting away in aimless rivulets.

Man, according to Duhamel, should bring all of his faculties into play in order to achieve happiness. Such a goal does not imply the eradication of the bitter in life. One cannot know one without the other. Pain must be experienced if joy is to be understood and assimilated. Suffering has its positive side since it encourages man to pass beyond this infernal stage, to look toward better things. There is nothing in life, Duhamel writes, which cannot become a source for happiness: farming, carpentry, scientific studies, business—whatever is undertaken by the individual must be related to his own life, his own development—his own soul. Only when a rapport exists, when the subject and object have made an *entente cordiale,* can happiness come to pass.

One of the most satisfying ways of arousing contentment in an individual is to develop within him the notion of helping others, sharing life with one's fellow men. Once he learns the meaning of "giving" of himself, he has discovered the capacity of that remarkable instrument which belongs to each of us: the heart. Once man is directed by his heart, life can assume more pleasant hues: "I hope that the heart will begin reigning, at the very time the old civilization is leaving behind the deathless traces of its murderous stupidities."[13]

The war experience, which could have been so devastatingly destructive to Duhamel's psyche as it had been to so many others, brought forth in him a deeper and more poignant realization of the meaning of life, a more striking sense of its beauty. His existence, therefore, took on greater scope, permitting him to develop values and concepts which he intertwined in his daily living experience. Duhamel hoped for a *rapprochement* between France and Germany, an understanding of the problems involved, an ability to permit the heart to speak out, to guide human beings in their various pursuits and in a concerted effort to work together toward a common goal which would benefit all of humanity. He wrote a short story "Carré and Lerondeau" (1922), which featured two soldiers recovering from their wounds. One said to the other, "Forget your leg, forget your martyrdom. . . . But the universe must never forget it."

CHAPTER 4

"My name is Salavin" [1]

T HE WAR YEARS, excruciating as they were, lingered on as a bad
memory. Fresh ideas, new enthusiasms burgeoned. In the novel,
old-fashioned Naturalism, Symbolism and Positivism were declared
passé. In their stead novelists searched for the revelatory, the indiscreet,
the intimate. These notions had now taken precedence and included
minute descriptions of the protagonists' meanderings in and out of two
realms: the conscious and the unconscious. Proust had abolished linear
notions of time and space in *Swann's Way* (1913). Gide had rejected
the literary and social status quo as early as 1897 in *The Fruits of the
Earth*. He was adamant in annihilating the family unit and to this end
preached fervor and abandon. Jules Romains illustrated his philosophical concept—unanimism—in his novel *The Death of Someone (La Mort
de quelqu'un)* (1913).

Foreign influences were also keenly felt. The Russians in particular
stimulated introspection, observation, analysis, and confession. Works
by Gogol, Dostoevsky, Tolstoi, Goncharov created beings dredged up
from man's lowest depths, incising them upon the reader's mind. These
creatures were forever struggling to keep body and soul together, trying
as persistently as possible, given their personalities, to prevent utter
submersion in the problems of life. Heroes conceived in this fashion
were no longer romantic creatures of fantasy rushing from one
adventure to another; rather they were ambiguous, labyrinthian
personalities, whose life processes developed into a series of antagonisms and conflicts.

Duhamel had definite ideas concerning the novel which he expressed
in his *Essay on the Novel (Essai sur le roman)* (1925). Though attracted
in his youth to the works of such Realists and Naturalists as Balzac,
Zola, Flaubert, Maupassant, he felt that with the inroads made by
science and psychology in the twentieth century, a new novelistic
quality had come into being: "psychological realism" The finest

techniques available to probe man's subliminal world would now be applied. In the nineteenth century when the Naturalists and Realists created their genres, geared to reproduce nature as accurately as possible, they used precise documentation as their tool. Zola, the Goncourts, Flaubert would either read the books necessary or walk the streets of Paris with notebook in hand seeking and noting the most precise of details. These innovators imbued their work with passion, imagination, and life. They were courageous and instructive in their endeavors. As time wore on, however, the fire of novelty and invention dimmed. The twentieth-century novelists who continued the Naturalistic trend became servile imitators. Documentation was transformed into a routine, perfunctory obligation. The result: an artificially constructed work, an intellectual exercise, superficial and of little interest.

For a novel to be meaningful, Duhamel reasoned, the events described should be authentic. The hero, for example, must be an outgrowth of the author himself; that is, he must have been experienced by him either symbolically or on a certain psychological level. The environment in which the protagonist lives and breathes must also be known to the author, so that he can react to circumstances in accordance with the region, the class, and so on. Since the hero is to be drawn in depth, his actions must result directly from his personality. Likewise, events and adventures must not be invented by the author, but must also fit into the framework of the entire personality created and the environment of which he is part. The picture must be a cohesive whole. Human experience, Duhamel pursued, is certainly vast enough to be able to pluck incidents truthfully from its storehouse, which is the world. If incidents are contrived, the final product is of little interest and, moreover, is utterly superficial. Finally, the plot, for Duhamel, is of little import. It is quickly forgotten once the book has been terminated; it is an exterior garment. What remains engraved in the reader's memory is the hero's impact upon him, his subliminal, mysterious, and hidden realm, which the author reveals slowly and forcefully by means of his X-ray vision.

The hero's character should be described in such a way as to compel both conscious and unconscious realms to exist side by side. In this manner, the reader may be able to project upon the protagonist, to become involved in the character's thoughts, activities, emotions, and sensations. This does not for a moment imply that the protagonist should be imbued with moral concepts, good or evil, or that he should adopt any particular moralistic attitude. Involvement should come about as a result of the impact the character has upon the reader; the passions he can resuscitate. His realm must rise up and confront or beguile the reader's world. The character, therefore, should be a representative type and inspire emotion: pity, fear, anguish, hope, admiration, or any other sentiment. Once feelings are aroused, the novelist has succeeded in his task.

Shortly before World War I, Duhamel wrote ten pages of what was to become the first of a five-volume series: *Confession at Midnight (Confession de minuit)*. In an essay, "Life and Death of a Hero of a Novel" ("Vie et mort d'un héros de roman") (published as part of *Two Employers* [*Deux patrons*], -1937), he details the genesis of this cycle, informing us that he had never had any plans for writing the work, that the hero, Salavin, was purely fictitious; indeed, the name was taken from Parisian chocolate shops.

Salavin, Duhamel declared, had at first imposed himself upon him and, as the years passed, had become more and more insistent until finally Duhamel felt compelled to externalize him on paper. There is no question but that Salavin emerged from Duhamel's unconscious and is, to a certain extent, an embodiment of several facets of the author himself.

In *Sowing in the Wind (Semailles au vent)* (1947), Duhamel informs us that the Salavin cycle was not architecturally constructed, that Salavin himself obeys the laws of life, that he is "the eternal man" who happens to be living at this juncture in the twentieth century. Though many people have called Salavin "sick," or mentally deranged, Duhamel has always resisted this interpretation. "The story of Salavin," he wrote, "is the story, generally speaking, of a failure."[2]

The Salavin cycle includes *Confession at Midnight* (1920), "Meeting Salavin Again" ("Nouvelle rencontre de Salavin"), a short story included in *The Abandoned Men (Les hommes abandonnés)* (1921), *Two Men (Deux hommes)* (1924), *Salavin's Journal (Le Journal de Salavin)* (1927), *The Lyonese Club (Le Club des Lyonnais)* (1929), *As He Was (Tel qu'en lui-même)* (1932). Duhamel, however, was not the inaugurator of the cycle novel. Emile Zola had written *The Rougon-Macquart,* a series of twenty novels which he himself described as the natural and social history of a family under the Second Empire between 1871 and 1893. Romain Rolland had published his ten-volume *Jean-Christophe* (1904–12), in which he related the story of a German musician traveling through his own country and France, observing and criticizing contemporary civilization, before Duhamel began his endeavors. Duhamel's Salavin cycle differs from the works of his predecessors in that he emphasizes the psychology of his character, analyzing his every thought, whether articulated or not, and pays little if any attention to the social aspect of his epoch.

I Confession at Midnight

Confession at Midnight is a profound and quite extraordinary study of an introverted man who cannot accept himself as he is, who is unable to relate to other human beings, who finds life absurd. Because of these variegated personality traits Salavin is difficult to assess and certainly impossible to categorize.

In certain respects Salavin is the direct heir of a hero type created by Gide, Radiguet, and the Dadaists. Gide, who always preached a doctrine of liberty and availability, embodied his beliefs in the insouciant and brazen adolescent Lafcadio *(The Vatican Swindle) (Les Caves du Vatican)*. Raymond Radiguet's heroes were also intoxicated with the thought of freedom *(Count Orgel's Ball)*. As for the Dadaists, they sought to break the barriers of convention in all of their creative activities, to destroy logic and reason and replace these with deliberate madness, intentional chaos. Jacques Vaché, a member of this group, committed suicide as a deliberate mark of his contempt for modern society. Once this "freed" hero type had emerged, bound to no code of ethics, no morality, no logic, he became the ideal after which much of French youth tried to model themselves. A void, as of necessity, then set in. Liberty is a goal to be sought when enchained. Once free, however, freedom must be put to positive use. Free for what? one might query. Otherwise, negativism, despondency and dejection set in, particularly when the hero is lucid.

Salavin is a so-called free hero. He is free from constraint, free from responsibility, but he is not free from his thoughts. Nothing has been offered to fill the emptiness which came with the birth of freedom. He has no goal in life, no positive way about him. He is a man incapable of action, devoid of a workable and realistic sense about life, unrelated to others emotionally, centered only about himself. Like Goncharov's remarkable hero Oblomov, Salavin spends his time in fruitless self-analysis which eventually leads to his own destruction and to the defeat of all those who surround him and love him. Salavin is the hero or antihero who precedes Sartre's Roquentin *(Nausea)* and Camus's Meursault *(The Stranger)*.

The plot of *Confession at Midnight (Confession de Minuit)* is uncomplicated. Louis Salavin, the narrator, tells his life story to a stranger in a bar at midnight. He has been fired from his job for having given in to an inexplicable impulse: to touch his boss's ear. Shocked, his employer screams, takes out his revolver, and threatens to go to the police. Salavin then returns home to the tenement he shares with his mother and informs her of his dismissal. On succeeding days he tries to find another job suitable to his personality, but is unable to do so. As the days wear on, he no longer even bothers looking for employment. Negativism permeates his whole outlook. He begins to lose his self-respect and deterioration ensues. His mother, with the help of Marguerite, a gentle and tender neighbor, takes in sewing to support herself and her son. Oblivious to his mother's long hours of arduous work, Salavin pursues his aimless wanderings about Paris. One day he meets a one-eyed vagrant, Lhuilier, who tries to help him earn some money. Salavin is deeply moved by this display of human kindness. He does not change, however, and is perpetually dissatisfied with himself. To relieve the monotony of his existence he visits his old and only true friend, Lanoue. Even this relationship is unsatisfactory, because when Salavin suddenly experiences a physical desire for his friend's wife, Martha, he is so shocked by his display of immorality that he is flooded with feelings of guilt. Without any explanation, he rushes out of Lanoue's apartment. Now he seeks to punish himself for his evil thoughts. He leaves his mother. He will do penance in his own manner.

Louis Salavin is immensely fascinating, an individual so involved in his own psychological conflicts that he is unable to see beyond them. His own turmoil stands uppermost; in fact, he wallows in it, and because of this psychological state his thoughts meander about in a circumscribed world. Introverted to the extreme, he is forever examining his lot, his ideas, his ways, his actions, in a most lucid and incisive manner. Instead of illuminating him, however, this self-probing merely increases his despair. His brooding, concerning his inability to cope with life's problems, increases as does his dissatisfaction with his own character. He describes himself as "larva, debris, residue."[3] The greater the dichotomy between the person he would like to be and what he considers himself to be, the greater is his despondency and morbidity.

Because Salavin is incapable of envisaging life beyond himself he cannot project upon people. He, therefore, feels nothing. Neither his mother nor Marguerite nor his friend Lanoue inspire any kind of emotion within him, certainly neither love nor hate. He is devoid of the ability to become and remain a friend and cannot muster sufficient will power or determination to amount to something in this "material" world. *Confession at Midnight* depicts in pitiful terms the slow and steady mental and emotional decline of the Salavin type.

Duhamel's technique for revealing the slow disintegration of a personality is twofold: first, by means of psychological analyses; secondly, by appealing to the reader's visual sense. In three separate episodes, comparable to three variations on a main theme, Salavin's utter shiftlessness, his weak inner structure, is brilliantly portrayed.

The first episode revealing Salavin's psychological state occurs when he touches his boss's earlobe. This is the only time in the entire novel when he gives expression to an impulse, transforming an amorphous thought into concrete terms. Such an act, when considered symbolically, has many ramifications. It indicates an intense desire on Salavin's part to feel the warmth of another person and the urgency with which he seeks to relate to others. The fact that he touches the ear—the hearing instrument—reveals his desperate need to speak and to be heard, his utter inability to exteriorize his thoughts. His extravagant and aggressive acts amount to a rejection of the social codes and indicate further the meaninglessness of bourgeois tradition. To touch a boss's earlobe is unheard of in this kind of restricted society. Once completed, however, Salavin's act does not bring him the release he had expected; instead, despair sets in. He has the impression of having completed a monstrous act. "I was exhausted, empty, vague."[4] Unlike Stendhal's hero, Julien Sorel *(The Red and the Black),* who confronts the social codes by touching Madame de Renal's arm and who feels utter elation and a tremendous sense of accomplishment after his act, Salavin experiences the opposite emotions—emptiness and, even, worse, guilt. Unlike Sorel's act, Salavin's is gratuituous: it is neither positive nor negative. It serves only to reveal an inner state and to set into motion the machinery which will lead to his degradation. Salavin's act is comparable in certain ways to Lafcadio's gratuitous killing on the train in Gide's novel, *The Vatican Swindle.* Neither Gide's hero nor Duhamel's has any *real* or *conscious* reason for acting as he does.

The second incident revealing an inexorable inner process of psychological erosion is Salavin's walk home from his office after his dismissal. He meditates upon how he can best confront his mother with the bad news that he has been fired. Fearing her many questions, her disapproval, her anguish, her solicitude, he imagines a thousand different ways of explaining rationally an irrational act. As he further probes and prods into his situation, he suddenly becomes irate. He is angry at his own indecisiveness and can no longer bear to accept responsibility for his condition. Like a child, he shifts the blame for his behavior onto his mother. Had she steered him in the right direction, he thinks, forcing him to study, choosing a métier compatible with his character, things would have been so different. By the time he reaches home, he has built up such an armory of reasons, stockpiled so many different emotions, that when his mother accepts the news of his dismissal in the most understanding of ways, without either questioning or blaming him, Salavin falls to his knees and utters sobs which come from his stomach, and which "unfurled like waves from the depth, chasing everything from sight, sweeping everything away, purifying everything."[5] A sense of release overcomes him after this onslaught of emotion and, with it, a return to the mother-child relationship which he has always known, save on that occasion when he touched his boss's earlobe.

Because Salavin has never evolved beyond the adolescent stage he is unable to function as an individual, as a mature being. He has always lived a peripheral existence, has never gone out on his own; for this reason, whenever he acts out of the ordinary, he is submerged with guilt feelings. His mother, gentle and kind, certainly not domineering, has created such a comforting atmosphere at home that Salavin never really attempted to carve out his own future. An indication of this tender mother-son relationship occurs after his sobbing, when his mother brings out the candies he loved to eat when he was ten years old. Salavin is comforted by them, as though he were reliving his past. Indeed, feelings of extreme security rock him and as they do, he regresses to the period of boyhood when everything seemed so right. Despite such moments of felicity, however, something within him begins to rebel. The more his mother babies him, the greater his "ferocious solitude." His subliminal realm is encroaching upon his conscious outlook. He seems to thrive on the utter privacy this world offers him—but not completely, since it does not bring him even the modicum of happiness an individual can expect from life. Indeed, his inner world frequently frightens him. His thoughts at times assume a sinister aspect revealing to him, he reasons, his own perverse nature. Such a reality frightens him. When, for example, he begins to meditate upon his mother's death, on the fact that he would inherit a small income, he is shocked by the baseness of his probings. He cannot believe himself capable of such a sordid view. In fact, he looks upon himself as his mother's murderer. Guilt invades him at such times. Then and only then does the reader become aware of Salavin's extreme morality. If he had not such profound notions of what is right or wrong he would never be party to guilt. Salavin is then further dismayed by the fact that he feels no emotional bond between himself and his mother, no energy to weep over the thought of her eventual death. Certainly Albert Camus must have read *Confession at Midnight* when he created his character, Meursault, in *The Stranger*. Here too a protagonist feels absolutely nothing when his mother dies. He is moved neither to pity nor tears nor laughter. He is devoid of emotion and merely continues his life as usual, swimming, working, and so on. His employer, his mother's friends, all look upon him as rather "peculiar" because he is devoid of all conventional and human ties.

The third incident revelatory of Salavin's inner state occurs during his visit to Lanoue. It is at this time that he begins to harbor lascivious thoughts vis-à-vis his friend's wife. Duhamel leads up to this incident in a highly intriguing manner: slowly, methodically, punctiliously.

We first meet Lanoue, one evening, when Salavin is visiting him and his wife, Martha. Salavin tries desperately to take part in the festive occasion, to be agreeable to his host and hostess, to communicate with them, to laugh at Lanoue's jokes. After a while, however, he finds himself encased in his own "tenebrous, impenetrable, deadly" solitude.[6] He can no longer respond to the feelings of his friends. He suddenly becomes terribly aware of the fact that they share no common denominator. This feeling of "separateness" grows, and as it does the tone of Salavin's conversation changes. It becomes tinged with irony and cruelty. He even manifests scorn toward Lanoue. Despite the few statements which emerge from his lips, he does control himself—indeed, to such an extent that he feels trapped. An uncontrollable urge to scream out seizes him. However, he does not yield to his desires; he keeps a tight clamp over his stifled emotions. He now senses vaguely that the reason he cannot communicate with his friends is due in part to his wish to dismiss or bury what he considers to be his own evil characteristics: laziness, negativism, egotism, coldness. Since he cannot accept himself as he is, he feels constricted. The limitations he places upon himself—to live up to the image he has created of himself—modify his behavior. He cannot act freely. He is, in effect, crippling himself. Thus far, however, he succeeds in controlling himself and in maintaining a certain amount of decorum. No one divines Salavin's real thoughts.

The second time Salavin visits Lanoue's house the situation is entirely different. Martha is alone. Salavin is suddenly overwhelmed by sexual feelings toward her. He controls them but with great effort. He is so submerged with feelings of guilt as he tries to master his thoughts, actions, and speech, that he rushes out of her house, feeling totally unworthy of any kind of friendship, his only desire to pay penance: humiliation of self.

Salavin's guilt certainly arises in part from his unconscious adherence to Jesus's dictum as stated by Saint Matthew:

Whosoever looketh on a woman to lust after her hath committed adultery with her already in his heart. And if thy right eye offend thee, pluck it out, and cast it from thee: for it is profitable for thee that one of thy members should perish, and not that thy whole body should be cast into hell.

Salavin has mistaken thought—something amorphous—for a concrete reality, the inner for the outer world, unconscious for conscious states, uncontrollable for controllable feelings. He feels a total responsibility for everything living within his subliminal realm. He is certainly well aware of his psyche as a living entity, but he is far from understanding it, evaluating its importance. This lack of knowledge leads him to reject those very elements within himself to which he should have paid close attention: his instincts. He rejects these so-called evil traits. As a result, they become more and more insistant, more and more demanding of his energies. Instincts, like animals ought to be well fed and contented: a starving animal becomes ravenous and ferocious; a well-fed one is pleasant and active in a positive manner. Had Salavin made an effort to understand what he considered a base trait (sexuality), he could have integrated this force into his whole personality. Instead of doing so, he takes Saint Matthew's advice and tries to "pluck it out" and "cast it from" himself. By suppressing the elemental characteristics or trying to eradicate them, one merely inflames them, adds to their power. Indeed, Salavin's instincts grow steadily stronger and emerge on unexpected occasions; namely, the ear incident, the sobs with his mother, the lascivious glance toward Martha. A psyche is neither regulated by the will nor by the mind alone—anymore than is a child, an animal, or a nation. If will alone is used to bind an individual to act one way or another, to crush his instinctual realm, then the monster within is sure to emerge. Salavin has never understood such a point of view. As a result, he fails to comprehend his own sexuality, his own spontaneity, and consequently becomes paralyzed at certain moments by guilt *feelings*. He is doomed from the start. Having taken Saint Matthew's statement for gospel, he becomes incapable of any positive act. He becomes a submerged entity, a lifeless being.

One of the most effective devices used by Duhamel to express his hero's utter negativism and goalless existence is the "walking" scene. Salavin spends days on end walking through Paris, preoccupied with his thoughts. He ambulates in circles, in the most perfunctory manner, detached from his surroundings, enmeshed in his inner realm. Symbolically speaking, his trajectory in life would likewise be circular, similar in many respects to that of Poprischin in Gogol's *Diary of a Madman*. In this Russian tale we are introduced to a character who also keeps analyzing his every move, his every thought, in the most lucid manner. Unlike this nineteenth-century protagonist, however, Salavin is not insane. Nevertheless, he is a haunted man, frightened by his thoughts and constantly rejecting aspects of himself. He is maimed.

Confession at Midnight is the finest volume of the Salavin series. It is a dense, analytical, highly stimulating study of a man's inner world. Few outside events mar the progression of the tale. Like a surgeon, Duhamel makes inroad upon inroad as he reveals, methodically, his hero's inner structure. Finally, he opens him up fully. At this point, readers can ponder, peer and postulate as to Salavin's future.

In the succeeding works, Salavin's personality does not change, though he undergoes a variety of experiences. Each episode serves to increase suspense, to reinforce personality traits, and to determine the unalterable course of an unbending point of view, to further test the inexorable nature of the protagonist's personality.

II *"Meeting Salavin Again"*

Salavin is next the protagonist of a short story, "Meeting Salavin Again" ("Nouvelle rencontre de Salavin"), the second time Duhamel introduces him to his readers. In this work, Salavin describes a theft he has committed, an attempt at suicide, a return to Lanoue's apartment and the seduction of his wife. Both his anguish and his guilt have increased to such a degree that he feels nearly desperate. His suffering is acute, comparable in a way to the anguish Dimitri knows in *The Brothers Karamazov*. When, however, the bartender, to whom he had related the *Confession at Midnight,* awakens him, Salavin realizes that what he has taken for reality has been *only* a bad dream. Relief sets in temporarily.

Though Salavin's destructive acts have been *merely* enacted in "dream" form, they still indicate the negativism and the aggressive tendencies present within his psyche. Rape, attempted suicide, theft are all acts geared against society, against humanity, and against self. Punishing the outer world—when he had tried to blame his mother for his own failings, in a previous episode—resulted from his inability to understand his own state, his imbalance, his deficiencies. After the extreme sense of deliverance sets in when he discovers the unreality of his acts, renewed dynamism is forthcoming. Salavin, relatively speaking, feels a certain sense of optimism and an impetus to begin life anew.

From a literary point of view, it is interesting to note that Duhamel clothes the entire incident in the dream. Certainly, this was intentional, not only in order to further the story line, to create excitement and suspense, but also because Duhamel himself was a firm believer in the *dream* as a revelatory instrument. In his autobiography he describes three unforgettable dreams he had as a child; he also discusses Descartes's very important dream, the one which led him to believe that God had given him a helping hand in the discovery of his mathematical principles and philosophical concepts.

Duhamel's first dream took place when he was still a child. He was downstairs, his mother upstairs, sick in bed, unable to move. She called to him to come up. He did not want to at first but finally acquiesced to her demand. Just as he was about to climb the wooden stairs all sorts of ferocious animals passed by the window opening: tigers, lions, and the like. They all had their jaws open ready to attack their prey. The child refused to go up stairs. In vain his mother called to him. He would rather, die, alone, downstairs than to pass through that jungle.[7]

In this fascinating dream Duhamel introduces us to the child's world, filled with fears, frustrations, and conflicts. The explanation of this nightmare is as follows. Duhamel sought to reject his mother's command, those orders emanating from "upstairs," from the matriarch. He wanted to be independent; yet he was very attached to his mother. Though something within him sought to disobey her commandment, the obedient-son aspect of himself won out. Just as he was ready to fulfill her orders, however, wild beasts made their presence known. They, in effect, impeded his march upward. Wild beasts, in this instance, represent instincts. They were there to stop him from "obeying" and to force him to "reject" his mother's command. Danger lurked every step of the way. Fearful of his instincts (animals), Duhamel remained paralyzed. His attempt at independence was realized, but through *fear* and not through wisdom. Yet, it is to be recalled, everyone's first attempt at "disobedience" is a terrorizing experience. Duhamel's example was no different.

In Salavin's dream we note also his desire to "disobey" society or to seek revenge upon this implacable entity. Unconsciously, however, Salavin's acts are overt and of a totally negative nature. In Duhamel's case, the child remains "paralyzed" with fear, not fulfilling his mother's expectations. In neither case is independence of spirit experienced.

III Two Men

Two Men (Deux Hommes) is a stunning study of friendship. Salavin has married Marguerite, the gentle seamstress who came to help his mother after he lost his job. Salavin and Marguerite have a son: a sickly child. One day, Salavin meets Edouard Loisel, a happily married man and successful chemist. They become close friends. Loisel finds a job for Salavin and tries to help him in every way he can, both financially and emotionally. When Loisel, for example, hears that Salavin's son must be sent to the seashore, he arranges for the lad's stay. The more successful Loisel becomes, the greater is Salavin's inability to share in his joys. He resents his friend's happiness and finally rejects it. They no longer see each other. When Salavin's son dies, Loisel, who is distraught over the break, sends his former friend a compassionate note of condolence, indicating his pain and implying that the breach between them is comparable in many ways to the misunderstandings which take place within societies and among nations.

Salavin has not changed. The first indication of this condition of stasis is indicated by the "sickly child," who symbolizes the outcome of an unhealthy relationship. He cannot possibly survive the ordeal of life because his father is essentially trying to maim and destroy himself. The latter is deficient in something and, therefore, is incapable of giving birth to a strong or vigorous progeny. As for the lad's mother, she is "bent" from the very beginning—both physically and emotionally. She represents the spirit and the essence of passivity. She has no life of her own, devotes all of her energies to her husband, who in no way really responds to her affection, and to her son, who is physically unable to take the "nourishment" offered by his mother since it is dispensed in too meager a quantity and too mild a dose. The child, therefore, withers as does a branch when deprived of sap.

The friendship between Salavin and Loisel is also doomed from the start. Foremost, Salavin is incapable of friendship. He has never known the meaning of such a relationship. His rapport with Lanoue ended in utter disaster. What comes naturally to basically well-oriented people can never be experienced by a man possessing Salavin's extraordinarily self-oriented personality. When Marguerite hears of Salavin's friendship, she is overjoyed, thrilled at the thought that, possibly, Salavin might be changing his frame of reference. Such communion between two men, she thinks, will certainly breach Salavin's solitude. In an intensely moving scene, Marguerite announces the good news to Salavin's mother. "Mother. . .Louis has a friend, a real friend, a good and faithful friend." "More than that, Salavin adds softly, a friend whom I love." Salavin's joy at this moment is boundless, his hope for the future enormous. He too then is swallowed up in the thought that personality changes, that man can evolve.

The Salavin-Loisel friendship is not to last. Unlike the seemingly "ideal" relationship enjoyed by Montaigne and La Boétie, based on mutual understanding and admiration, the Salavin-Loisel rapport emerges from diametrically opposed forces. It is based on misunderstanding. Salavin symbolizes the introvert, the suffering, the pained, the masochistic. Loisel, on the other hand, represents the extrovert, the happy fellow who has never experienced any kind of anguish. Loisel feels a keen sense of joy when he realizes he can be of help to Salavin. Such feelings of satisfaction, which arise each time he accomplishes a good deed, are due in part to his need to dominate. Loisel is certainly unconscious of any desire to keep the upper hand in their relationship. He really never thinks about the situation and looks merely at the "act" itself, rather than at its motivation. He would be incapable of introspection anyway, since his thoughts are all directed toward the outside world, never to the inner being.

As the friendship becomes more and more intimate, so Loisel acts in an increasingly paternalistic manner. He is always "acting" for the welfare of his friend. Salavin, therefore, leads a passive existence, becoming the recipient of all the good works. Loisel goes so far as to try to prevent *all* suffering on Salavin's part, to endeavor to alleviate life's destructive processes; unwittingly, he is eradicating the fight necessary to daily life, the spirit of competition for advancement. To deprive an individual of the dual nature of life—its share of joy *and* of suffering—is to stifle him. Salavin feels this handicap. He can never share in his friend's world, nor can he live out any kind of experience with him, fruitfully, as an independent human being. Salavin begins to resent his subservient role.

Other factors enter into Salavin's growing dissatisfaction with his friend's attitude. He is jealous of Loisel's success. He becomes angry with himself, with his own deficiencies, with his meek and weak existence. He begins to blame Loisel for his own lacunae, for his inability to grow or to achieve something in this life. His jealousy begins to gnaw at him; his sense of inferiority increases in arithmetic progression. Feelings of rancour become so strong as to prevent any positive act on his part. Indeed, he decides that a total break with his friend is the only way in which he—Salavin—will be able to evolve as an individual. He is in many respects sincere in his appraisal of himself. What he does not realize is that he will never flower, never bloom as a human being; he will continue to remain imprisoned in his own claustrophobic atmosphere.

After this incident we are exposed to another view of Salavin: his feelings. Whether he admires them or not, he does possess feelings. He does suffer, and most intensely, after the breakup. He does feel pain and is no longer the detached human being he thought he was. Marguerite becomes aware of this aspect of her husband's nature as he sleeps one night with his fists tightly clenched, and two tears trickle down his cheeks, between the hairs of his beard. Salavin is wrong when he declares his inability to *feel* deeply toward others. His feelings have become so repressed because his resentment toward others and toward himself has taken precedence over everything else in his psyche. Indeed, with him sentiments have become virtually nonexistent. Only when asleep, when the rational mind no longer dominates unequivocally, is suffering visible.

Loisel is also an interesting personage. He has to "do good." He needs to share his happiness with others, to live a life outside his family unit, to fill his hours with extreme activity, to build, to create. Such frenetic activity indicates, of course, a void within his own makeup. He has never experienced pain or suffering. When the break with Salavin occurs, he feels cut off, empty, drained of life's force. Now, however, because he has experienced another aspect of existence, now that he would know life as whole, perhaps growth may occur. For the first time, Loisel is forced to look within, to contemplate his acts, his feelings, his entire frame of reference.

The kind of friendship enjoyed by the protagonists in *Two Men* cannot, as we have seen, be prolonged. It is based on an unconscious will to dominate, the need of one to thrive on the other. In effect, one member has to be the parasite. True friendship has to be experienced individually; each member must be independent of the other and bring all aspects of himself into play in such a relationship. Because friendship *can* thrive and on the highest of levels—as an interchange of ideas and feelings—it can be a fructifying experience, a force capable of enriching two lives. This "ideal" type of friendship, however, can only be enjoyed by those whose personalities are already well integrated and balanced. Loisel and Salavin are actually two facets of but a single being: Loisel represents the outer core, Salavin the inner. Neither can understand his own needs and is certainly unable to cope with them. Only after the breakup is it possible for either to try to become a fulfilled man.

IV Salavin's Journal

Salavin's Journal (Journal de Salavin) (1927), written in the form of a diary, broaches the question of sainthood. Salavin, now forty years of age, is determined to become a saint and decides to devote all of his energies to this task. He leaves his mother and his wife and spends all of his time in a concerted effort to help others. He evidently has not learned from past experiences. Just as he was resentful of Loisel's paternalistic attitude each time his friend sought to help him, so those toward whom Salavin now aims his kindness are equally annoyed. In his office, for example, one of his co-workers, Jibé Tastard, steals some of the office's petty cash. Salavin replaces the money each time with funds from his own pocket. Finally, after Jibé is fired, Salavin still keeps giving him money, though he can ill afford to do so. On another occasion, Salavin tries to help his landlady, then a drunkard. In each case, his kindness remains unappreciated. When Salavin learns that the milk company for which he works does not pasteurize its milk as it claims to do, he writes a letter to the police, declaring naively that the public is being cheated. His boss does not fire him when he learns of the incident, but gives him a job in his office in order to watch over him and his future "moralizing" attempts. Another time, during a panic in a theater, Salavin runs out of the building as fast as his legs will carry him without attempting to assist anyone. When he meditates upon his flight he recognizes the difficulties involved in becoming a saint. He now considers himself a coward. At the end of the novel he begins to look toward organized religion as an answer. Here too he is disappointed. The Protestant pastor whom he seeks out is in reality more of a businessman than a spiritual force; as for the priest, he is not only uninterested in Salavin's confession but cannot even begin to really understand it. Salavin does meet a young priest, Abbé Pradelles, who prays with him, and he considers this man a saint. But he comes to the conclusion that as far as he is concerned, religion offers no solution. He was and is an unbeliever. Despite such an outcome, he is still intent upon reaching sainthood—in a moral sense, not in a religious one—and as a last gesture before abandoning the entire idea, gives his only coat to Jibé Tastard whom he meets on a cold evening in Paris. Salavin catches pneumonia and enters a charity hospital.

Salavin's Journal is particularly interesting, not only because of the form of the work itself, but because of the psychological ramifications involved in Salavin's desire to achieve sainthood.

The diary form which Duhamel chose—in the manner of a Rousseau or of a Gide—was designed to take the reader into the protagonist's confidence, to permit him to see directly within the character. The attempt is successful. No detail is spared in Duhamel's deft dissection of his hero's ideas, sensations, or reactions. Words that are never uttered, merely surmised, live freely in this fluid, fast-moving realm. For example, Salavin wants to keep his goal secret from everyone. Therefore, he substitutes the word "tourist" for the word "saint" in his diary. Later, when he becomes aware of the infantile nature of such subterfuge, he simply writes "S." These machinations, however, indicate Salavin's inability to be fully honest with himself.

Salavin's desire to reach a state of sainthood is not the result of intense faith on his part, but rather of extreme vanity. He seeks to be different from others, to live in a secluded world, to be *greater* in this respect than his fellow man. To become a saint, however, usually indicates a desire to reject the world, a wish to transform oneself into spirit, a negation of the flesh. In essence, to become a saint is to annihilate the physical or carnal side of humankind and to cultivate man's so-called godly aspect. If one succeeds in becoming a saint one can escape from everything considered "base"—of the flesh—and live in the upper spheres of an idealized realm. If Salavin had been a saint he never would have coveted his friend's wife in *Confession at Midnight,* if he had been a saint he would have been a giver and not a taker, as he was in *Two Men.* Salavin's intent to become a saint is a cerebral decision, as indicated in his diary: "Today, on January 7, my birthday, I am resolving to transform my life totally. . . ."[8] and "I must become a saint. This is the only thing which still depends upon me alone."[9] His entire personality does not participate in this decision. It is his mind, his reason which seeks to dictate his choice. Like the stoics of old, Salavin believes that man's "animal" nature can always be kept in check or even destroyed by his "reason." Again, his endeavors will be doomed to failure.

Salavin's notion of sainthood, as we have seen, has nothing to do with the church per se. There is no religious dogma whatsoever involved. He admires saints in general for their virtue, their ability to conquer their passions, and he seeks, therefore, to become a simulacrum of them: charitable, kind, while at the same time destroying his own manly side. He feels that slowly he is progressing in his discipline. Such a realization is firmly felt when he begins helping Jibé. He confesses that he has now opened his heart to a man he would formerly have despised and shunned.[10] He also feels a sense of accomplishment—a step upward in the ladder toward sainthood—when he "courageously" writes a letter to the authorities revealing the milk company's dishonesty. On this occasion he notes the following in his diary:

A marvelous day! The experiment has been performed. The results surpass all my hopes. To have unmasked the guilty party, is little; but I revealed myself to be the man I had hoped to be when beginning my ambitious quest. Ah! nothing is lost! Perhaps Salavin will reveal himself. Salavin will do great things, perhaps.[11]

This statement gives the reader a clue to Salavin's true intentions. His self-centeredness, his utter vanity are the motivating forces behind his urge to become a saint. He seeks admiration; he wants to draw attention to himself to gratify his ego. This implication is further attested to each time he completes a so-called act of kindness. He experiences moments of extreme bliss, invading not only his conscious existence but his unconscious world as well. At night he is "haunted with exalted dreams. He dreams he is flying away, and by means merely of a simple effort expended by his will."[12]

Salavin's quest for sainthood reveals even more poignantly the solitary, wretched, and unhappy existence of this man who cannot accept himself as he is, who cannot really observe himself with honesty. He is a man whose feelings have been so frustrated, whose sentiments so blatantly curtailed, that he finds himself utterly unable to act spontaneously, freely, naturally. He must, therefore, build an edifice to give his life structure and point. His edifice, however, is top heavy because it has no solid foundation. It must, therefore, crumble.

Since Salavin considers the attainment of sainthood a matter of will power, that one need merely flex the will as one does a muscle, his downfall occurs as a result of a peculiar incident. His wife, by mistake, closes the door on his fingernail. Salavin screams. He suffers great pain. Then he suddenly realizes that a saint would never have cried out in such a manner. A saint would have buried his pain, rid himself of passion in every form and completely eliminated the world of flesh, of desire. Salavin is now aware that he has failed in his mission, that he is essentially a man without faith who must go his way alone. "Each individual must shift for himself, alone, in his hole, in his garbage. And moreover, I have no faith."[13]

V The Lyonese Club

In *The Lyonese Club* (1929), which is the least interesting volume of the series, Salavin becomes involved with a group of revolutionaries, Communists, and fellow travelers. They meet in the cobbler shop of an old idealist and revolutionary who wants to set the world aright for his dying daughter. Salavin admires some members of this group for their sincerity and their humanity. However, when it comes to a test of these so-called idealists, he realizes that in no way do they live up to expectations. A check must be cashed by someone who is not known by the authorities to be affiliated with the party. Courage and selflessness must be expended at this moment. Aufrère, who has always preached objectivity and detachment, decides, for reasons of vanity and much to Salavin's disappointment, to go through with the heroic deed. Devrigny, another member of the party, discovers he has syphilis and, despite Salavin's attempts to console him, commits suicide. The police finally locate the members of the group, arrest them, and even search Salavin's apartment. When his mother learns of the situation, she is so shocked she dies of a heart attack. Marguerite is stunned, bewildered by her husband's incomprehensible acts.

From a literary point of view, *The Lyonese Club* is a "thesis" novel. In Duhamel's attempt to show up the Communists for what they are, he dispenses with the important stylistic device: his analytical study of Salavin. The book is overly involved with politics; there are far too many secondary characters introduced into the work; and the story line is complicated and detracts from Salavin as the central figure. The many characters in this volume are never described in depth; they are, therefore, fragmented, tiresome, and peripheral.

Salavin, we learn, has not evolved. Indeed, he seems to have regressed. Moreover, his story now seems of little interest to the reader. He neglects his family, as he had formerly, and attempts to take part in another "project," a political one this time. He feels as he did before, when he first wanted to become a saint, that if he succeeds in becoming a fine "Communist," as a member of the Lyonese Club, he will create another being from the raw material which is self. He again fails in his attempt. At the end, before leaving his wife, he says: "If I triumph over the world about me and over myself, if one day I consider myself robust enough so that I will no longer fear my own phantoms, I will return and knock at your door."[14]

Marguerite assumes greater importance in this novel, not because her presence is described in detail, but for the humanity and compassion she shows her husband and others. She suffers her fate in silence. She is the real martyr, the saintly creature Salavin had sought to become. As she looks at herself in the mirror, she realizes that she has become an old woman, poor because she has no husband, no children, no friends. She is indeed, a woman without a story.[15]

Salavin, a strange and enigmatic figure, has admitted to his weaknesses. He can do nothing to remedy them. He tries to flee, to carve out another world for himself. There is no salvation for such a one—merely doom.

VI   As He Was

As He Was (1932) is the last of the Salavin series. The title for this volume was drawn from Mallarmé's sonnet on Poe; it has, therefore, profound meaning. It implies that Salavin will finally unmask himself totally, will live out his existence truthfully at the end, painfully. We find Salavin traveling on a train to Tunis under the name of Simon Chavegrand. In his compartment he meets Louis d'Argoult, his wife Gertrude and their child, also going to North Africa. As the train pulls into Marseilles and the passengers alight on the platform, the child, unnoticed by her parents, wanders off on the railroad tracks. Salavin sees a train coming at the child. He rushes toward her and saves her from death at the risk of his own life. The parents are extremely grateful. Once in Tunis, Salavin tries to continue his heroic deeds by curbing the evil ways of his assistant Arab boy, by caring for patients in the hospital, by exposing himself to typhus in order to test a new vaccine. His endeavors, however, though altruistic in appearance, are fruitless because they are motivated by selfish reasons. He does not help humanity for love of his neighbor. The situation reaches a climax when his assistant is wanted by the police for criminal activities. Salavin tries to persuade him to give himself up. It is at this point that his assistant shoots him in the leg. The wound becomes infected. Marguerite is summoned from Paris. Salavin's leg is amputated. He and Marguerite return to Paris and there he dies while lying on his couch.

One can feel Gide's strong influence in this novel. The location of the story is North Africa, the seat of Gide's *The Immoralist,* as well as of other works. What is even more Gidean, however, is Salavin's supposedly "gratuitous act" when he saves the child from sure death in the Marseilles railroad station. Gide had also included an incident of a "gratuituous act" in *The Vatican Swindle,* where the hero, Lafcadio, kills a passenger in the compartment of a train for no reason whatsoever. Salavin's act, however, unlike that of his contemporary, is a positive one, since he saves a life. In neither case, however, can one really know whether the act is truly unmotivated. Salavin could have been satisfied with his act because, for the first time in his life, he brings joy to those around him. He truly helps humanity. He acts in a saintly fashion, committing a deed for someone else—while risking his own life in the attempt. Gide's hero, self-centered, has no feeling for others; he is totally amoral, beyond convention, beyond life in general.

One of the most arresting features of *As He Was* is Duhamel's use of the train as a symbol. Gide had used this machine with felicity in *The Vatican Swindle;* in more recent times, the novelist Michel Butor has done so in his novel *The Modification.* A train usually indicates a means of escape from troublesome reality or from a world of constraint. For Salavin it becomes a means of entering a new land, another existence, to feel light and lithe, to wipe away one's sins. Salavin is going to North Africa to enter a world he considers harmonious and warm, to bask in the hot sands, to bathe in a natural atmosphere. As the train's journey comes to an end, so must his thoughts of escape. Salavin recreates for himself a very nearly identical situation in North Africa. He seeks to become a saint, to be a dispenser of good, to outdo himself in his service to humanity. Again he refuses to face himself, to discover the reasons for his actions. His leg is amputated, symbolically speaking, in order to force himself to stop running away, to end a life of shifting goals and of aimless meanderings. Each individual must finally face himself one day, assess and evaluate his own thoughts and acts. At the end, Salavin does so. In Paris he looks back upon his existence and is convinced that if he had his life to live over again he might know how. "How simple it would be! How happy we would be! " He tells his wife.[16]

Salavin has finally learned to better understand both himself and the forces about him, to accept the differences between overt acts and unconscious thoughts. Man is responsible for his actions but not for his inner wanderings. An enormous difference exists between the thoughts one harbors and the manner in which one transmutes these in daily life.

Saint Matthew's dictum had created a horrendous state of guilt within Salavin, which he had forever sought to assuage.

There is no question but that Salavin—the character—preoccupied Duhamel increasingly ever since he made his first appearance within the author's psyche before World War I. In a touching epilogue to *As He Was,* Duhamel wrote that Salavin had become his friend:

Sleep, sleep, poor man! Sleep, you, my friend, my unhappy brother. Withdraw into nothingness, companion of my youth and my more mature years. You have really sufficiently suffered by my hand, and I also add, for me. You have, for so many years, suffered sufficiently within me. The time has now come for me to abandon you, now that evening is coming upon us.[17]

The Salavin series is a soul-searching work. Its sincerity, its eternal qualities, its universal characteristics, its simple and straightforward style account for its popularity. There were critics of course, as there always are, who disliked the work for its negativism, for its lack of religiousness, for the hero's "selfish" manner: John Charpentier, Gabriel Marcel, and others. Most readers, however, were touched by Duhamel's powerful creation, by his tremendous capacity for suffering, his humanity and his desire to alleviate the burden of guilt which plagued him throughout his existence. These readers demanded more and more volumes from the author.

It might be said that Duhamel had felt compelled to pursue the Salavin cycle after the end of World War I, not only because his public demanded it of him, but because it was a release for his own sufferings. The extreme activity expended and the tension sustained by Duhamel during those gruesome war years had not yet been calmed. His emotions were still taut; turmoil lived within him. His home life, his children, his writing brought him joy and fulfillment. There were other moments, however, when alone, that he indulged in introspection, in self-examination. Within him some of Salavin's characteristics might be smoldering, and Duhamel set out to try to evaluate these within the frame of some creature of his fancy. Once brought to light, once Salavin lived as a flesh-and-blood human being, Duhamel could evaluate his creature's characteristics in the light of his own personality. In each of the volumes he tackled another phase of Salavin's life: friendship, sainthood, political affiliation, the gratuitous act. Duhamel bored deeply within the self, trying to understand man more completely through his egoism, through his generosity—by any means.

The Salavin cycle can be considered a polyphonic work, because the several variations and harmonies interwoven into the series all emerge from a main theme—the hero. Each succeeding interpretation or every act on the protagonist's part is sounded out by a medley of undertones and overtones, always accompanied by lugubrious background sounds.

CHAPTER 5

Levels of Reality

DUHAMEL, the *pantophile,* was fascinated by every phase of life. His approach to existence was eclectic. It was as though he were reaching out to all branches, to all manifestations of life, whether physical or amorphous, emotional or intellectual, in an attempt to *possess the world.* Little escaped his attention; very nearly everything that came under his scrutiny elicited some kind of reaction from him.

Because he was swept up with life in general, by the same token he could not limit himself to one art form. The novel was as yet not sufficient to capture his full attention. He branched out, chose other vistas, other means and ways of expressing his burgeoning ideas: short stories, novels, essays (on art, politics, travel), works of fantasy, inspired by a variety of people (his children, nieces, nephews), and articles covering many subjects including music.

I *Short Stories*

As a short-story writer Duhamel donned his magnifying lenses, sharpened all the tools at his disposal which would help him observe his surroundings more accurately, and became a devotee of *le mot juste.* In each of his stories, he first outlined the situation in general, then set about filling out the various phases of the action. Uppermost, however, were the characters. These were pertinently described, in short, pithy sentences. Exteriors were focused upon first; then the surgeon-writer reached deeply into the interior of his creatures and, from there, viewed the world about him, discovering a more profound and meaningful reality: "This region of reality has its believers, of which I am one. It can even boast of having its fanatics, which I prefer not to be."[1] Once the characters had come into full view, they lived their existence boldly or fitfully, pitifully or cruelly, according to their natures and environments.

Duhamel, as has already been stated, was particularly interested in studying the human heart in its most sordid, cruel, and tender aspects. His vision of human suffering, noted in his war books, is again brought to the fore in his short stories, but in a different manner, frequently through satire and irony. He displays, moreover, a great flair for building suspense, a talent for creating an atmosphere of fright and awe. These devices were virtually unnecessary in his war books, since the subject itself was sufficiently horrendous and gruesome.

The title, *The Abandoned Men (Les Hommes abandonnés)* (1921), which Duhamel chose for his first volume of short stories, is indeed apt. The men whose lives he depicts and etches so forcefully on paper are all "abandoned" souls, rejected by society in some way, incapable of relating to others, solitary, inexplicably aggressive and introverted. They might have been, to some extent, outgrowths or prismatic views of Salavin, a phase in his development, caught up by the author and placed in another environment to live out a different story. They are, for the most part, either evil in intent or the victims of some cruel act. The peasants, whose world is highlighted in these tales, are vicious in all of their overt as well as unconscious acts. They are ready, in virtually every case, to kill another human being, if not physically, then psychologically, and without an afterthought. The lonely, the shiftless, the weak are perfect targets for these evildoers. What is of extreme interest, however, is Duhamel's preoccupation, in this period, with questions of *evil*. It must have been the natural outcome of the clashes he had witnessed during World War I, the intense and collective confrontation between nations, with hatred as its most salient feature.

Stylistically speaking, Duhamel's talent for storytelling is never better displayed than in *The Abandoned Men*. The humble lives of ordinary people are dramatized with objectivity yet with great warmth, but the treatment is never maudlin, even under the most gruesome of circumstances. The contrast in personalities, as well as the nature descriptions which frequently mirror the characters of the protagonists, make for powerful effects.

The tale entitled "The Carter" ("Voiturier") deals with murder. The pathetic cobbler, Landrel, is a man who has never known a moment of joy in his entire life. Always led by events rather than a leader of them, he suffers the iniquities of a society which has rejected him. Worse, he is not articulate. This speech defect may have resulted from feelings of inferiority, from the belief that he is not wanted, that he serves no purpose in his home town. Since he cannot seem to express himself properly he is blamed for a murder he never committed. Though proven innocent, he is nevertheless considered guilty for several other crimes committed in the region.

Strangely enough, though there is only one flesh-and-blood Landrel, two distinct types emerge from this story. The first is the real man whose life remains an utter mystery and agony to the townspeople. This unfortunate, pathetic human being has been ostracized and is forced to live in the most primitive manner on every meager savings, since no one will hire him. The second is the legendary Landrel. This figure has in effect been created by the overwrought imagination of the inhabitants of the village. In their minds, he is an ominous figure, without doubt a murderer. Unable to communicate with anyone, failing to vindicate himself from the guilt placed upon him by the populace, the flesh-and-blood Landrel, pathetic and lonely, wastes away and passes into oblivion.

"The Origin and Prosperity of Monkeys" ("L'origine et prospérité des singes") is one of the most arresting stories in this volume, imbued as it is with the acidulous humor of a Maupassant, a Mérimée, a Flaubert, or a Zola. A doctor's experience is related. In the small town in which the story occurs, it is rumored that the product of an incestuous union is not the stillborn child claimed by the girl involved but rather a monkey. The doctor tells of this strange happening with scientific calm and detachment, making the pitiable situation that much more frightening. The doctor, afraid of telling the truth—that a stillborn child has come into the world— and fearful of facing the townspeople's anger, since their minds have already decided on the "monkey story," finally comes to believe his own lie. He is, therefore, an accomplice to the vicious calumny. Once he yields to popular opinion he relates the story once again, describing the monkey he has delivered: it wears glasses and it eats coconuts. The doctor even goes so far as to attest to the truth of the story: "I can give you my word of honor, since I am the one who brought it into the world."[2]

In this tale, Duhamel has captured, with extraordinary precision, man's intrinsic cruelty, his basic weakness, his fear of fighting the mob. Indeed, the doctor is not strong enough to stand the villagers' anger, which he fears he will arouse if he should not go along with their concocted tale. The pettiness, the narrow-mindedness, and the innate brutality and ruthlessness of the French peasant—a group unto themselves—are analyzed with strength.

"The Wreck" ("L'épave") deals with man's greed. A cargo ship has been washed up on shore. The villagers rush to the sailing vessel with baskets and all types of containers, to take what they can from the abandoned hulk. In their mad quest for material goods, mothers leave their squealing tots, workers their labor, priests their pulpit.

Nothing, Duhamel implies in this tale, is to be feared more than man's possessive instincts. With clarity and vigor he paints man's slow degradation in terms of his lust for gain, achieving a stinging effect by contrasting man's rapacity with the poetry of the wind, the breathless beat of the water and the pounding rays of the sun—all cleansing and healing cosmic forces.[3]

II *Novels*

Though at work on the above-mentioned short stories and on the Salavin cycle, such activities did not prevent Duhamel from completing several novels and an *Anthology of French Lyric Poetry from the End of the Fifteenth Century to the End of the Nineteenth Century.*

A German publisher from Leipzig asked Duhamel to prepare an anthology of French poetry for German readers. He had always felt that a *rapprochement* should be effected between France and Germany, and he wanted to participate actively in such a venture, through cultural means. So with this in mind he prepared an anthology and declared in his preface that it contained only masterpieces, poetry of the most beautiful type, subtle music of and for the soul. Every kind of poem is included, from the most celebrated lyrical works of Villon, Baudelaire, Vigny, Musset, Nerval, Hugo, to the least known works of Marguerite de Navarre, Saint-Evremond, Maucroix, Colardeau, Malfilatre, and others.

Duhamel was fortunate indeed. He was not only versatile but wrote with extreme rapidity. His ideas seemed to flow forth, coalesce, and set themselves down on paper with ease. It must not be construed, however, that he had no method or technique. On the contrary, he followed his own discipline, which he later outlined in *Remarks on Imaginary Memoirs (Remarques sur les mémoires imaginaires)* (1934).

Literary endeavors are to be based on real-life experiences, Duhamel suggested, this being the only authentic manner of writing. The world, filled with infinite mysteries, is rich enough, he maintained, to be an eternal source of nourishment for the creative mind. Reality, however, must not be presented as is; it must be offered readers with artistry, sobriety, and reserve. Duhamel further elaborated: everything introduced into a novel must be related and intertwined and must create a type of *fondu* from its disparate parts, of which truth becomes the alpha and omega of the entire work.[4] A literary endeavor must grow like a tree, have a solid foundation, give off strong shoots which eventually grow into firm and beautiful branches.[5]

Duhamel never set down any detailed techniques for writing. Each author, he believed, must find his own reality and express it in simple and forceful terms. Prose, he intimated, should follow the rhythms of respiration, and since each writer is possessed of his own mechanism and personality, his work will have its own individual tempo. The sound of prose must likewise be varied, as is its meter. Tonal structure should include the variegated ranges implicit in the human voice. Prose, consequently, must possess the differences present in nature as well as its measured harmonies.

The Prince of Jaffar (Le Prince de Jaffar) (1924) is a work difficult to categorize. Strictly speaking, it is not a novel, nor is it an essay or a travelogue. It has the trademarks of each of these types. In it Duhamel relates, with clarity and objectivity, his impressions of Tunisia and the influences that country has undergone. Moreover, the volume serves as a stepping stone, a device which permits the author to examine in detail the various historical landmarks still existing in this land of sand and heat.

Unlike André Gide, who found joy and freedom in North Africa, whose stay there symbolized both psychological and physical liberation (as described in *The Immoralist* among other works), Duhamel sojourned in this land strictly as an observer, noting down, as he visited the various areas, as scrupulously and objectively as possible, his impressions of the customs, the philosophies, and ideologies of these desert-surrounded people. Nor does Duhamel's *Prince of Jaffar* resemble Pierre Loti's exotic novels set in Constantinople (*Zilade,* 1897) or in Japan (*Mme Chrysanthème,* 1888), whose sensual style is so imbued with melancholy overtones. Simple and unadorned, Duhamel's intention is not to underline the differences existing between Occidental and Oriental civilizations but rather to depict man and his customs as he observes them, both outwardly and inwardly. When watching a veiled woman walk about the marketplace, for example, or a man in a burnoose, Duhamel leads his reader on—ever so gently—to examine the inner realm, thoughts, beliefs, the very souls of these people.

To read *The Prince of Jaffar* is to take a giant step back in time, to revisit a civilization gone by. The people who fall under the author's scrutiny are not cerebral and mechanically oriented beings, as the modern European thinks of himself, but rather the primitive, the natural being, whose entire psychological framework leads him toward adopting a different outlook toward life, death, and divinity.

In the first pages of Duhamel's volume the reader learns that the Prince of Jaffar is having a house built, that the chief mason Mokrani has been ordered to present his plan before the bureau of hygiene. Duhamel then takes the reader into Mokrani's house to visit his five children; to the doctor who delivered them all; to the Prince with his numerous wives and offspring, his worn brocades, his fourteenth-century manuscripts. A plethora of anecdotes and vignettes follow concerning the ideal servant Habib who is respectful, docile, dreamy; the young married couples, some of whom are happy and others who have experienced misfortune and pain (wife-beaters, cuckolds, etc.); the Jewish community with its strict mores, its extreme poverty, and its persistant idealism in the face of all adversity. Various superstitions are also included in this volume as well as tales, such as that of the dolphin who became conceited, so reminiscent of Rudyard Kipling's *Just So Stories.* Details of architecture, houses with and without patios, gardens, and olive trees are described; notions on prisons, epidemics of cholera, fleas, filth, and hygiene are also accurately presented.

Duhamel succeeds in arousing his reader's interest through his sensitive portrayals of so many types ranging from the penurious to those wallowing in luxury and joy. His local-color tones, his images so sharply incised, enhance the meaning and flavor of this volume. It might be added that Duhamel's compassion, as always, comes to the fore, in his feelings of pity for the suffering and his anger directed at the oppressors who take advantage—everywhere and at all periods—of the less fortunate, the weak, and the ignorant.

Horeb's Stone (La Pierre d'Horeb) (1926) is a novel in every sense of the word, one in which Duhamel focuses on a profession he knows thoroughly—medicine. The story concerns Antoine Rességuier who comes to Paris from nearby Ferte-Milon to study for this profession. A hard-working student, he holds on to the sincere ways of a country lad, even though in the big city. His attitude toward women is naive and certainly adolescentlike. For this reason, perhaps, his infatuations with both Daria and Anna end in disappointment and heartache. He suffers from extreme loneliness, which increases after he realizes that many of the Russian medical students with whom he has been keeping company are far more interested in Communism and Karl Marx than in their own biological studies. He looks upon these politically oriented individuals as hypocrites. When he is faced squarely with the hard facts of reality, he feels all the more isolated and despairing.

What stands out most vividly in this novel is Duhamel's ability to depict his protagonist's feelings of solitude in terms of nature. He succeeds in drawing from a large expanse of sky, from plateaus, trees silhouetted in space, feelings which correspond to those experienced at that particular moment by Antoine:

> When I travel on the roads of the plateaux, in April, I love to stop my car at some intersection, to savor the solitude there. The sun frees space for one minute from the clouds, thrusts its tongue out on the land sown with crops, and each blade of grass immediately exudes its own perfume.[6]

Though *Horeb's Stone* is in many ways autobiographical since it describes Duhamel's own school days, his work in the laboratory, his rapport with his co-workers and co-students, it gives, nevertheless, an impression of artificiality at certain times. A contrived tone is most apparent when dealing with love episodes. Duhamel seems hampered, even prudish, when trying to depict feelings of love and sensuality. This may be due to his lack of experience in writing about this aspect of life. Because he fails to yield to a spirit of abandon, the novel as a whole is marred and does not seem authentic.

The Stormy Night (La Nuit d'Orage) (1928) which varies considerably from Duhamel's previous novel, is one of his most fascinating works up to this time. It is exotic in nature and, because of the excitement it generates, it brings to mind Théophile Gautier's *The Romance of the Mummy* and Balzac's *Wild Ass's Skin (La Peau de Chagrin)*. More than titillating the senses and the imagination, however, *The Stormy Night* dramatizes a certain psychological state which we refer to today as psychosomatic illness.

François Cros and his wife Elizabeth, a chemist, have both been brought up in a scientific atmosphere, where the mind, not the emotions, dominate. After returning from a short trip to Tunis, they show their anthropologist uncle a souvenir—an amulet—they have brought back with them. The uncle informs them that it brings bad luck and warns them to discard it. The couple scoffs at such a statement. Shortly afterward, however, Elizabeth falls ill. Hers is a strange sickness, whose symptoms are weakness, lethargy, and a lack of interest in anything and everything. Both Elizabeth and François, though they have never discussed the point, feel inwardly that the amulet is working its mysterious and nefarious powers. Eaten away by this suspicion François decides to throw the object away. He looks for the monstrous amulet but cannot find it. He is convinced it has been discarded. Now that the couple believes it is no longer in their possession, Elizabeth suddenly recovers. When cured, François happens to find the amulet buried under some clothes in one of the bureau drawers. Concomitantly, he receives a letter from his uncle, indicating that he had made a mistake in his description of the amulet: it really is the harbinger of *good* luck. This news serves to reinforce the couple's feelings concerning superstition in general. Now, however, they realize to what lengths the mind can go in developing anguish in a person's psyche, in wearing him down and ruining his life. The peripheral characters (brother, cousins, etc.), some of whom are agnostics at the beginning of the novel, become religiously inclined at the end. As for François and Elizabeth, they are thrust into a state of extreme confusion, aware now that neither *extreme* (the overly scientific and rational or the unduly religious and superstitious approach) is valid. Balance and harmony must reign.

The question of scientific rationalism versus religious faith preoccupied many writers of Duhamel's generation. Claudel, in 1895, admitted that his excessive enthusiasm for Taine and for scientific attitudes in general had led to his reconversion to Catholicism. The overemphasis on the cerebral and rational always causes its opposite to take hold at given times, as it certainly did to several of Duhamel's contemporaries: François Mauriac, Jacques Maritain, Charles Péguy. Rather than examining events and emotional problems in the light of scientific analysis—which was Duhamel's method—these deeply religious writers veered sharply toward the mysteries present in the universe as an explanation for everything, submerging to a certain extent in so doing their critical and rational faculties.

Duhamel opted for balance between the two extremes: science blended with feeling and understanding of human problems and needs. As a doctor, he realized full well that to undervalue one facet of man is to overvalue the other; both are dangerous to human welfare, and polarities in general are deleterious to social evolution. Drastic attitudes and concepts serve to strangulate the individual and in so doing prevent him from fulfilling himself and his destiny—prohibit him from *possessing the world*.

What seems most striking in *The Stormy Night* is not the

development of the characters described, though these are well drawn, but Duhamel's interest in psychosomatic medicine. When the mind—all-powerful—is obsessed by some fear or anguish, it can play havoc with the rest of the body. Had the idea of "evil" not been implanted in the couple, Elizabeth's sickness might have been considered something natural and, though unpleasant, could have been coped with in a less negative manner. Once the mind had been enticed into a destructive direction, however, it was no longer free to search, to examine the situation analytically and so became prey to a phobia. Had the belief in the amulet's power persisted, the couple's lives might have been ruined under the weight of such a negative ideology. It is most interesting to note that the reason the belief in the amulet's power possesses them with such vigor is that a breach existed within their own psyche: the rational function had been overfed while the emotional aspect of their world had become undernourished. Only when imbalance reigns can such obsessions take hold. The confusion in the couple's attitude at the end of the volume permits a reshuffling of thoughts and concepts and, therefore, an incitement to new points of view—a replenishing thereby of the undervalued side of their personalities, paving the way for eventual balance.

A person succumbing to any extreme cannot hope to live a well-balanced life. To be anchored irremediably to one's belief is to reject conflict. Conflict or antagonism is part of existence and, when experienced in a positive manner, leads to growth and evolution. Peace, on the other hand, is a condition of stasis, and is incompatible with life if life is to be lived fully. Change must occur as does a heaving breath. Realizing this important fact, Duhamel wrote: "I enjoyed reasonable peace; I disdained it. I had certain certitudes: I abjured them one by one."[7]

III *Essays*

The essay form also served Duhamel well. It became a splendid vehicle for his biting irony, satire, and jocularity. In *Auspasian Letters (Lettres d'Auspasie)* (1922), for example, he introduced to his reading public a series of essays ranging from discussions of the theater to scientific subjects—"On Orators," "On Scientific Mores," "On the Theater," and so on."[8]

Whether Duhamel levels his sarcasms at orators, who are so narcissistic as to have become infatuated with their own voices; or at those who are overly gullible and believe anything and everything, falling victim, thereby, to the stentorian voices of self-proclaimed gods; or at those who are convinced that life's problems can be answered with simple formulas and so succumb immediately to various political groups (whether leftist or rightist), without applying reason and logic to their attitude—his slings and arrows always penetrate deeply. Life, explains Duhamel in "On Some Adventures of the Mind," is a constant struggle with the elements as well as with people. Applying understanding, however, when faced with difficulties, helps solve them and in so doing permits people to live fully and completely. Those who are convinced that pat answers are for the asking and that these can explain the complexities facing man, are indeed misguided.

Writers, likewise, face insurmountable problems not only in terms of the effort each author expends when creating the work per se but after it has appeared in print. If a volume is well received, detractors are ever present, venting their disdain in the most strident and bellicose manner. Success arouses jealousy, and threatened destruction resulting from such tangled emotions must be coped with and overcome by the author who is experiencing the butt of hatred.[9] To inure oneself to castigations is not a simple task. It requires strength and vision.

Though the literary and scientific world always attracted Duhamel, he never once forgot his war experiences. These had so traumatized him that they had altered his entire attitude toward life. Indeed, he felt that the horrendous aspects of the war—as gruesome and painful as they might be—should be kept before the public's eye. He was convinced that torture, blood, gore could be instrumental in helping pacifists such as he to avert another conflagration. Who would want to suffer? Who would want to inflict pain? For this reason, every now and then, Duhamel produced a work treating of the war and its aftermath. Let man contemplate his own destructive side, the devastation he has wrought, then perhaps he will work for peace.

In *The Last Seven Wounds (Les Sept dernières plaies)* (1928), Duhamel takes his readers back to the World War I period, to a hospital at the front where he had been a surgeon. He recounts, with an irony and a bitterness tinged with pathos—always with extreme understanding—certain case histories: the colonel who, though cured of his wound, refused to leave the hospital; the old-time army man who could not get along with the modern volunteer; the pitiable soldier who had suffered wounds in his chest, thigh, and throat, and who when he drank almost strangled because the liquid he imbibed kept pouring out of his nose and through the hole in his throat.

War, however, was not the only aspect of life against which Duhamel fought. In *Pages from My Journal (Pages de mon carnet)* (1931), a group of essays which had appeared in newspapers and magazines, he lashes out at millionaires and materialists, at a society which gives so much credence to technocracy, to "psychology" based on that "evil-doing magician" Freud, at doctors who remove the human element from their practice of medicine and who rely solely on the objective machine to perform their medical miracles.

Duhamel, however, was never one-sided. Whenever depicting the sordid aspects of modern society or humanity in general, he always counterbalanced his literary endeavor with its opposite, man's eternal search for serenity, his notions of joy and well-being. Duhamel, who reacted so deeply to the beauties of nature, responded equally forcefully to the canvases of Maurice de Vlaminck. He appreciated the turbulence and the violence which his friend, Vlaminck, injected into his landscapes, and noted these in an essay, *Vlaminck* (1927).

A representative of Fauvism, Vlaminck rejected the traditionalist approach to art. His paintings are highly original outpourings which seethe with feeling for everything that lives and breathes, which react to the tremendous movement as well as to the softness of line and color tones intrinsic to the objects that came into his view. Vlaminck, Duhamel wrote, does not seek to shock either the bourgeois or the aristocrat. He tries to paint his vision of the world without recourse to theories or preconceived notions. He works from the inner being or entity outward, through feeling tones, by means of the affinities which exist between subject and objects: canvas, brushes, paint—all materials used by the artist. Such a technique is obvious in his painting *Snow at Epiais,* in which the vagueness of the sky, the road, and the house form an ambiguous quality which arouses the deepest and most turbulent sensations in the onlooker. In his landscape, *The Road to Butry,* this same arresting quality lends a mystical tone to a landscape which acquires distance as one gazes at it, which becomes cloudy and dreamy as time goes on. Vlaminck's canvases are action personified, and Duhamel succeeded in rendering this feeling—as well as the spirit of the painter's work—in his essay.

Duhamel not only enjoyed observing the variety of landscapes depicted by Maurice de Vlaminck in his canvases but also his still-life paintings: a bottle of wine, a tablecloth, bread set firmly upon it. This attraction for simple and natural things made Duhamel irate over what he considered artificial and overly complex. He frowned upon the overindustrialization and the loss of individuality which plagued society as he saw it. Duhamel was one of those who revel in the pride and joy of achievement: a beautifully constructed shoe, the aroma issuing from baking bread or of slowly cooking jams. He also experienced pleasure in the beauty and comfort of the home and the security which issued from feelings of well-being implicit in family life. He therefore deprecated a society which relied wholly upon the machine rather than upon the individual. He feared the downfall of civilization—and in a not-too-distant future—if man were to continue to pursue such a course as frenetically and blindly as he appeared to be doing in the 1920s.

Duhamel was not alone in expressing such a negative view toward man's scientific, technical, and industrial gains. In novels, essays, plays, and films, similar views were intimated and uttered by others, as for example, Jean Giono.

As early as 1901 H. G. Wells had expressed his own ideas on man's future in *The War of the Worlds* and later in *Things to Come*. He was convinced that scientific advances were totally outdistancing man's intellectual and social development. Charles Chaplin also caught this idea and satirized it over and over again in his film, *Modern Times*.

In 1923 Karel Čapek wrote a fantastic melodrama entitled *R. U. R.* (Rossum's Universal Robot), in which he describes civilization after it has been taken over by the machine. Just as the automatons or robots (a word coined by the Czech author) are about to conquer the human race, they turn into human beings and save the world from annihilation. Man at the end conquers the machine and forces it to act on its behalf rather than permit himself to be tyrannized by it. The play dramatizes the fear that technological potential will finally destroy man, that life without struggle will do away with all incentive within the human being and will thereby debilitate him and imperil his survival.

Aldous Huxley in *Brave New World* (1932) depicted a grim picture of the world in the year 632 A.F. (After Ford), in which scientific development has led to a dehumanization of mankind. Human embryos, he declared, will be developed in bottles and brought up to live passively in a collective world.

Duhamel expressed his anxieties concerning similar trends in *America: The Menace, Scenes from the Life of the Future (Scènes de la vie future)* (1930), *The Twins of Vallangoujard (Les Jumeaux de Vallangoujard)* (1931), *Family Quarrel (Querelle de famille)* (1932), and *The Humanist and the Automaton (L'Humaniste et l'automate)* (1933). In these works he examines sorrowfully the disappearing values of what had once been known as "civilization" and deprecates those who are destroying what he loved so deeply.

Scenes from the Life of the Future is probably the most violent attack on overcommercialization and overindustrialization that Duhamel ever wrote. It was completed shortly after he had returned from a brief visit to the United States (1928), a visit which included stops at New Orleans, Chicago, New York, and several other cities. In many respects this anti-American diatribe, as many people have labeled it, is quite a superficial work in that there is no attempt to evaluate the positive and negative accomplishments of a young people. Furthermore, it reveals an utter skimpiness of knowledge of both the country and its inhabitants. On the other hand, *Scenes from the Life of the Future* is a valuable work in that it foretells certain problems with which the United States is faced today: racism, the lack of incentive displayed by Americans, the destructive aspects of a welfare state in which the people are convinced that the national government owes them a living and the inhabitants owe nothing, a land in which work seems to have become a stigma, effort, an insult.

From the very moment Duhamel set foot on the American continent, he seemed to resent everything about this machine-dominated society where individual effort has been abolished and incentive decried. He had only one hope, he wrote: that Europeans would not seek to emulate Americans. He ridiculed, and with bitterness, the fact that visitors from foreign lands had to pass quarantine, were compelled to have their temperatures taken, their eyes examined for trachoma, and had to submit to a series of embarrassing questions. Once on terra firma, Duhamel expected to view beautiful landscapes and panoramas. Instead, he was struck by the ugliness of his surroundings: garish signs, advertising billboards all designed to mar the esthetic senses, smoke emanating from innumerable factories, garbage heaps dotting the horizon, automobile graveyards every few miles, privately owned forests surrounded by barbed wire, thereby preventing the people from enjoying peace and tranquillity.

America had become offensive: a dirty land given over to merchants, certainly no longer a source of inspiration for poets or painters. Moreover, everything seemed to emerge from a common mold: apples, pears, eggs—even women's legs—were constructed and shaped on an assembly line. The word "variety" had evidently disappeared from the American way of life. Food, people, clothes, architecture—thinking—everything was the same. Duhamel, an individualist par excellence, wrote: "I belong to a people of peasants who for centuries have been cultivating fifty different types of plums and find each one to be possessed of an incomparably delicious taste."[10]

In addition to the uniformity which is characteristic of the United States, Duhamel noted, with perhaps great exactitude, that Americans never take pleasure in eating. They are so calory-conscious that they cannot sit down at table in a relaxed manner and savor the dishes placed before them. They are always in a rush; no sooner do they sit down than they rise and leave. They never seem to have time to finish anything or derive any real joy from their sundry activities. Forever rushing here and there, into crowded elevators, cars, buses, planes, Americans never waste time. "Time is the greatest of riches," he noted, "and you never have any."[11]

What perhaps revolted Duhamel most deeply was his visit to the Chicago stockyards. He called this realm "the kingdom of death." He was greeted there with groaning and bleating animals, with cries of anguish and pain, because animals were slaughtered in the most merciless manner. The dust, the smell, the killing en masse seemed, ironically enough, "inhuman." Because of his utter aversion for this state of affairs, he labeled Chicago "The Tumor city! The Cancer city! The monstrous city!"[12]

There were other aspects of American civilization which Duhamel was to condemn: the car, which he felt had killed all desire to walk. The result: physically, Americans will become the most lazy people in the world. The auto, it has been said, has conquered space. Duhamel affirmed that it has also ruined it because it has done away with silence, solitude, and beauty. It has filled open spaces with disconcerting noises, gas fumes, and the like.

The film industry fared no better under Duhamel's swiftly stinging pen. Films crush any feelings of creativity on the part of the viewer. "The very dynamism intrinsic to cinema tears away the images upon which our thoughts would like to alight."[13] Pictures pass at such a quick pace in front of the viewer that he can never become bored with what he sees; his imagination is forever being bombarded by all manner of visual and vocal effects. One must know boredom, Duhamel asserts, in order to learn how to relax. Boredom can be a very positive force; as each being seeks to flee from it, he develops initiative, self-control, inventiveness, and effort. Americans, for the most part, he reasons, sit back and let the film industry take over—or any other machine—while they remain totally *passive*.

There is no question but that certain of Duhamel's conclusions were a bit hasty. His stops in the United States were limited, and, when visiting the areas under discussion, he did not make a concerted effort to talk with people, nor to visit libraries, museums, or universities. He spent most of his time in factories, in stockyards, or in his hotel room. It is also true that he had preconceived notions concerning the United States before he ever set foot on the continent. Such an attitude certainly marred his vision. Nevertheless, many of his statements have proved to be true. Not merely have technocracy and overindustrialization become a horrendous reality, not only has man become enslaved by the machine—still worse, the individual has been destroyed in this collective society. He no longer prides himself on achievement, nor does he work hard to accomplish something which will help fulfill him as a human being. A new kind of person has been born: one of the most nefarious types, emanating from the philosophy basic to the "welfare state." The new citizen of this land sits back and receives, is convinced the world owes him a living. Laziness, a total unwillingness to work on any terms, corruption have taken hold of what had once been a burgeoning land. Such a state of affairs can only lead to the decline of a country which, in its early days, had struggled so hard to achieve mightiness.

When Duhamel returned to France he wished, he declared, that he had never set foot in America. It had depressed him frightfully. He warned his countrymen of the evils of machine mania and hoped they would stay away from this type of culture. He was not very sanguine, however, about his own country's future. Men are men, most probably, the same every place. In The *Twins of Vallangoujard*, a bitter satire replete with humor, Duhamel attacks his own country and its inhabitants for already having been caught up in the frenzy and fury of mechanization and uniformity. He cringes for the future!

Duhamel had not yet said his last word on the subject of modernity. Indeed, he had been relatively restrained. Now, more aggressive in *Family Quarrel,* he castigated modern civilization as a whole for its creation of a one-sided world and of top-heavy human beings. He was not suggesting by any means a return to the Middle Ages or an escape into the wilderness or an idealization of the "noble savage" state which Jean-Jacques Rousseau had so vaunted. He suggested, rather, a slowing down of technocratic developments and industrial advances so that man could catch up emotionally and morally.

Family Quarrel is not a cerebral treatise written against the ills plaguing society. It is a satire in which Duhamel, with tongue in cheek, suggests that national parks, for example, be built so that people could enter them for a small amount of money and dwell in an atmosphere, at least momentarily, free from turmoil, noise, and the odors of modern life. In Duhamel's youth, he adds, the small towns in France were safe from these gruesome aspects of life, so jarring to the nervous system. Now, however, in 1931 (when this volume was written) the machine and its side effects have invaded the remotest regions of France: trains, cars, radios, planes, phonographs, trolleys, loudspeakers.

Modern man, Duhamel asserts with a wry smile, takes great pride in the cleanliness of his towns, villages, and cities. He fails to observe his twentieth-century achievements: the filth permeating so many areas which are used as industry's dumping grounds, the waste products filling the rivers, polluting the waters, killing the animals and all esthetic sense. Cities have become staggering masses of dirt and garbage. Horizons have disappeared because of the smoke emanating from the factories and from all sorts of chimneys. Machines and industry have so overwhelmed every phase of modern existence that Duhamel wonders whether church sermons will eventually be delivered through loud-speakers, whether confessions will be recorded, whether all rapport between worshiper and priest will vanish.

In Duhamel's opinion man has lagged so far behind, emotionally speaking, that he has reached a point where he virtually personifies the machine. This can be attested to by his treatment of his car, his electric iron, his motor launch. A modern citizen spends hours on end hovering over his favorite mechanical toy, examining it with unparalleled solicitude. To treat and consider a machine as one does another human being indicates that something in man's psyche is lacking, that something within him is terribly defective.

It is because Duhamel loved the present, his land and the world in general, he confessed, that he felt compelled to point out the ills: "I have only one desire, one goal: to seize, to embrace, to paint the present period, which is the source of my wealth, my part of eternity."[14] For this reason, he felt that a moratorium should be placed on inventions for a while so that man—inwardly at least—could catch up. Were Duhamel alive today, he would be dismayed to learn that what he had foreseen had come to pass: that waste products from factories have caused river pollution, that an overly noisy world has contributed to deafness, that smoke emanating from factory and car fumes have caused lung cancer and other related diseases, that television and various visual media have brought about a state of intellectual laziness in many, that uniformity has done away with individuality, that the welfare state has given rise to indolence and idleness, both of which breed vice.

In *The Humanist and the Automaton,* Duhamel, the doctor, analyzes the pathology of the machine-guided civilization. Man, Duhamel explains, is the only animal who has done away with the tradition of instincts; that is, he has attached his organism to a machine. As a result, he has become decadent; he has abdicated all "incentive." He no longer writes but typewrites, refuses to use his head to add but has recourse to an adding machine, will not walk but rides instead. In medicine, for example, the doctor is now a specialist only. His relationship with his patient is no longer close. Because he relies so completely upon the machine when making a diagnosis, he no longer uses his imagination, his intuition, his feeling values. Nor does he try to build up the patient's morale, which is a veritable healing factor in itself, by talking with him, trying to understand him in his time of need. As a result, man is more isolated than ever. Human contact has vanished. Warmth no longer exists. Duhamel does not deny the positive attributes of the machine but decries man's overreliance upon these instruments. Because of their one-sidedness, the machine has become a destructive force.

Duhamel feared the creation of a society of robots, of impersonal beings. Indeed, he was certain that the trend toward depersonalization, toward abdication of all incentive and effort, would permeate all professions in time. The teaching world would not escape this fate. The human being responsible for molding the mind of future generations would be replaced by "radiophonic-cinema." Duhamel was not against this kind of visual aid, if it were used in conjunction with the human element. Not one *instead* of the other.

It was not really the machine per se which he castigated, since he had a car, a telephone, electrical equipment of all sorts, but the misuses of these, their proliferation. "It is the discipline of effort," he wrote, "which permits man to aim always higher, to constantly confront new and more difficult tests."[15] He was distressed to think that books would be relegated to the background while films, the radio, and records would assume enormous popularity. The proliferation of matter and the diminution of spiritual values frightened him. He felt oppressed and depressed when he became aware of the dangers lying ahead for mankind: the utter imbalance within society between matter and spirit, between the individual and the collective. The future, for Duhamel, looked bleak, indeed.

IV *Travel*

Despite his pessimistic view of things to come, Duhamel strove hard to learn more and more from the world in general and its people in particular. He was, therefore, a great traveler. Though his trip to the United States had saddened him considerably, there were lands he had not seen and which he wanted to visit, not only for personal reasons, but because he had great empathy for their people and also as a learning device.

Duhamel's visits to foreign lands would always follow a certain pattern. He made it his obligation to note what he saw, to question inhabitants, to read journals and newspapers if he could or to have them translated for him. He tried in every way possible to immerse himself in the various cultures with which he came into contact. As a young man he had hiked throughout France and Switzerland. After the war he had journeyed to Italy, North Africa, Poland, Czechoslovakia, Germany, Russia, Finland, Belgium, Holland, and, as already noted, the United States.

Czechoslovakia thrilled Duhamel (1925). What aroused his sympathy most forcefully perhaps was the spirit of democracy which seemed to permeate every aspect—the very "soul"—of this people. He wrote about their idealism; he reacted to their sincerity almost instantly. There is no question as to the affinity which existed between him and the Czech people.

Duhamel's trip to Finland and to Russia inspired *The Song of the North (Chant du Nord)* (1929), which he later published in the volume entitled *Cordial Geography of Europe (Géographie cordiale de l'Europe)* (1931), along with essays on Holland and Greece.

Duhamel was impressed with Finland, this small land submerged for so many days in darkness and in rain. The sharp contrasts in color inspired a variety of sentiments ranging from melancholia to a sense of excitation: the stark whiteness of the snow-covered fields, the brilliant greens of the forests, the black rivers as they flowed briskly down the mountain slopes. The wisdom of the Finns, a hard-working population, also appealed to Duhamel. They seemed to mirror their sturdy, handsome landscape. The majestic pine trees standing erect and strong symbolized, for Duhamel, the Finns' invincible nature—tall, thin, supple: "Countries resemble man: they degrade or exalt, by the very fact they exist."[16]

Duhamel's trip to Russia was less elating. He was not as objective in his notions concerning this country. Though he visited museums, hotels, theaters, schools, and libraries, trying to remain as truthful as possible, he could not help deprecating Communism for its dictatorial methods, the restrictions it imposed upon intellectuals and their pursuits. Those who think and create, he wrote, must suffer the ignominies of humiliation in this Communist land. Young authors have been *ordered* to write "realistically" and on certain subjects. As for painters, their lot is no better. They must picture workers and industry in a land where the laborer is deified. The same can be said of the pedagogical system in which the government "has merely lent the features of a new liberty to former servitude."[17] Such a state of affairs is not only intolerable, Duhamel claimed, but dangerous.

Duhamel did not overlook the fact that Communist Russia did bring about vast improvements in the material welfare of its people. The lot of the common man had certainly been raised. In other areas, however, little progress had been made; rather, there had been retrogression—in the arts, in particular. Duhamel was prophetic on certain subjects; namely, when he stated, most categorically, that the lot of the Jews would be no better in Communist Russia than it had been under the Czarist regime. People who could indulge in pogroms, he wrote, would continue their career of annihilation in another form. Such people cannot become humanitarians overnight. Jews the world over, he insisted, are deluding themselves if they think for a moment that anti-Semitism is dead in Russia.

When Duhamel returned from Russia he delivered a speech, later published in *A Conversation Concerning European Spirit (Entretien sur l'esprit européen)* (1928). He questioned whether there was such a thing as European spirit. He could feel one emotion blossoming throughout Europe: *hatred*. He felt that Europeans must work this emotion out of themselves, they must make a concerted effort to save the Occidental civilization which is so close to decay. World War I, he continued, had enfeebled the European countries and created a climate of anger. Internationalism, brotherhood among nations should be the goal of each European. To be "citizens of the world," Duhamel wrote, was his wish for all involved.

When Duhamel visited Holland he came away with a totally different impression from the one he had had in Russia. Freedom and liberty breathed in every aspect of this society; its beautiful fields, cities, ports, farms, dikes, flowers, and people inspired him with feelings of peace and repose.

In Greece, Duhamel was captivated by the fables and myths as well as by the monuments to culture standing all about this land of magic and beauty. It was here, he reminisced, that the Delphic oracle voiced her prognostications, that the poets and artists of antiquity molded their works of eternal beauty. It was here also that the bacchantes yielded to frenetic orgies. In this land of stunning contrasts—the blue of the sea and the whiteness of the land—Duhamel experienced an esthetic feast.

In *Alsace Perceived (Alsace entrevue)* (1931), a charming book illustrated by Duhamel's friend, Berthold Mahn, he captured the quality of this country's forests, lakes, magnificent cities (Colmar and Strasbourg), cathedrals, squares, bridges, and boats. This region, Duhamel contended, had not yet been shorn of its beauty by an overly industrialized society. Animal sounds could still be heard resounding through the countryside and the landscape was still relatively free of soot and grime, the wind still pure and free of factory odors.

Duhamel's travel books on the whole are fascinating not only from the historical point of view, for included in them are the most important facts concerning the lands in question, but because of their social and esthetic values. The countries visited are described with a painter's eyes, lending vividness to the entire volume. Moreover, Duhamel's perspicacious comments on the mores of the various inhabitants, the cultural differences, the goals and ways of the peoples involved, and what he divines as the future of each of these territories, point to the depth and precision of his intuitive-type thinking.

V *Children*

Duhamel not only had a feeling for nature and for people in general, but his greatest love was perhaps directed toward his own family: his wife, his three sons, and his nephews and nieces. Duhamel's gentleness, his solicitude, his entente with those "little beings," as he called them, come to the fore. For this reason, the works he devoted to children are among his finest.

Pleasures and Games (Les Plaisirs et les jeux) (1922), subtitled *The Memoirs of Cuib and Tioup (Les mémoires du Cuib et du Tioup)*, nicknames he had given his two older boys who were then six and four, respectively, takes us through the joys and tribulations of parenthood. Duhamel describes his children in all phases. His son Bernard, as he plays in the garden, walks along the country paths or in the streets of Paris, learns through his taste buds, since he insists upon picking up anything and everything he finds and putting it directly into his mouth, with the delight or disgust only a child knows when discovering a new sensation. Duhamel also marvels at a child's particular brand of logic, so deeply entrenched in him. When, for example, his son is thirsty and demands water, if no water is to be had, he still does not take no for an answer. He demands water because the adult's refusal is not logical. Duhamel further marvels at the sincerity of these little beings, at the fertility of their imagination.

There is no question but that Duhamel veritably revels in father-hood. He describes, with utmost glee, the unparalleled joy he takes watching his son sleep at one year of age, outdoors in the country during the month of May. He observes him as the little being inhales the warmth of nature and the purity of the air, strengthening agents, adding to his well-being. Duhamel's feelings burst forth in these passages and his sense of excitement and contentment is extraordinary.

When portraying children, Duhamel is able to catch their every aspect in one or two strokes, like a drawing. One scene is unforgettable. When his son has a bad dream and cries out in anguish, he and his wife rush to the child's room with dread anticipation. They find nothing out of order. "Sometimes, from the depths, there rises a slight noise: a sign from the little sleepers, a laugh or a word extracted from the dream." Duhamel confesses that as a doctor, he is frequently overly concerned about the welfare of his children. The slightest accident or sickness occasions the worst of anticipations. When, after a physically exhaust-ing day, the children are firmly tucked into their beds, both mother and father breathe a sigh of relief. They know that at this point most of the dangers are nonexistent and they could now relax.

Feelings of anger are also aroused in Duhamel, for example, when one of his sons is given a cannon for a gift. Duhamel and his wife decide to let him accept this weapon but to store it in the attic. They are antiwar and feel strongly that this kind of toy—a symbol of destruction—should not invade their domain. "Why not," he suggests in jest, "give them a guillotine?"[18]

The Erispaudants (1926), a charming and fanciful work, ac-companied by Georges Bruyère's woodcuts, was written after watching his children at play. Duhamel depicts a very special society—a group of people called Erispaudants, brought to life by his children's imagina-tion. These beings (certainly mirror images of the children) look upon themselves as belonging to a different race, smaller in size, adhering to mysterious customs and whose exploits are legendary. The Eris-paudants, for example, eat everything, even buttons; they dig holes all about the garden and fields; their language is characterized by repetitions of certain syllables, an arbitrary syntax and a rather small but expressive vocabulary. The Erispaudants wage war every now and then, and when they lose to another group, "The Messieurs" (certainly the adults), they have to follow orders. When punished, they are placed in one of the designs on a carpet and must remain there until their oppressors permit them to move. Many times, however, the "Messieurs" forbid them to touch certain objects about which they are told they know nothing. "The study of the Erispaudants frequently gave me great insights into the rest of the world, other men and myself."[19]

As for children's education, Duhamel felt it was a two-way affair. In *My Kingdom (Mon Royaume)* (1932) he describes such a situation. He was inspired to write this work when he saw his own children building a veritable city-state, to their dimensions of course, right in back of his house. He discovered that a division of labor existed in their society, but no restrictions had been set upon vision and effort. Moreover, he learned that no matter how young the children were, there was always a leader and a follower, certain aptitudes displayed in terms of emotional or rational attitudes toward given situations. Duhamel was convinced that theoretical treatises on child upbringing should not be written unless the author himself had been a parent and had experienced the joys and concerns which those little people afford one. Moreover, he felt that parents should carefully observe their children, contemplate their activities, grant them sufficient liberty to evolve as individuals, encourage motivation, develop memory, and always set up certain restrictions as a frame of reference. All education, he maintained, must be based on love and understanding.

As a father, he expresses in the most loving terms the fleeting joys and moments of rapture that his babies and children, later on, afforded him:

I look at my little man and as a passionate witness I say: the day will come when they [my children] will remember nothing of this marvelous period of childhood. Since they have hardly any help, nor have they any means, nor perhaps even the desire to make their present knowledge known to us, there is an abyss, an entire world buried within them.[20]

VI *Music*

Music also afforded Duhamel intense joy and relaxation. He always enjoyed listening to classical works, even as a child. He took up the flute in a serious manner in World War I, during moments of respite between operations. It soothed his jangled nerves, forced away his depression, and brought him extreme contentment. Throughout the years, music became an intrinsic part of his life, as important to his welfare as food and fresh air: "It is the key to all life, the one and sole enrichment of life."[21]

When writing, Duhamel had recourse to musical descriptions to render emotions and sensations much more vivid. In *Civilization,* for example, when he sought to describe death wreaking its havoc, he wrote, "A violin, accompanied by a piano, played a Bach sonata. Together they suddenly attacked the adagio part, filled with a poignant majesty. I had the impression, on several occasions, that an invisible and unknown person was placing his hand on mine, murmuring, 'How, how can you forget he is dying' " The music had forced forth certain feelings deeply immersed in the protagonist's unconscious, to the light of consciousness. Solemnly, steadily, and surely, he was finally able to face the glaring facts.[22] On other occasions, Duhamel outlined musical phrases to portray nature in its various manifestations or the sounds of cities at certain times of day.

When writing of food Duhamel included musical descriptions. In some of his works he depicts certain dishes as having their own harmony or polyphony. Some foods, while cooking, remind him of certain compositions because of the aroma which emerges, the staccatolike sounds in the heating process. From some dishes there emanates a classical, almost sacred tonal quality: grains, temperatures, and everything connected with this culinary art, take on the richness of a prolonged and melodious note.

Music, for Duhamel, was a source of release, a liberating force from all the constraints imposed upon him by society and by himself. In 1921, his friend Albert Doyen asked him to speak at the Fêtes du Peuple. Duhamel did so. He spoke not only of his love for music but of the fact that music makes for a much fuller and richer life. Love of music can be acquired. Duhamel's speech was published with the title "Liberating Music" ("La Musique libératrice").

Duhamel felt a particular affinity for Bach. About his work, he wrote years later:

I affirm that he is my life's companion, whose presence at my side I feel to be as real and often more real than that of any living person. I say that he is my guide and friend who alleviates my travail, enlightens my darkness, answers my most secret thoughts, encourages me and hears me as I gropingly make my way through the shadows and phantasms of our incomprehensible world.[23]

The Bach cantatas accompanied Duhamel through his anguished period during World War I, through his happy days when the holocaust was over and he lived a family life. It was in this period that he began to play Bach's Brandenburg Concertos, with flute, piano, and other instruments. Such heavenly music supplemented the joys he experienced in his wordly existence: "Bach's work is so magnificent and rich that it responds to every movement of the soul in every circumstance."

CHAPTER 6

The Pasquiers and Worldly Order

THE NOVEL FLOURISHED in the 1930's. It seemed to have been given added impetus by such writers as Duhamel, Colette, Mauriac, Romains, Martin du Gard, Bernanos, Montherlant, Saint-Exupéry, and Giono. Though some of these novelists — post-Realists — continued to pound out their works in the same general mold, relatively speaking, as their ancestors, recounting objectively and in precise details the happenings which came under their scrutiny, they imbued their volumes with new points of view, altered vision.

The post-Realists sought and succeeded in depicting the lives, the passions, the thoughts, and the ideals of families or individuals whom they had encountered in their daily existences or who had inhabited their world of fantasy or both. The atmosphere they created for their protagonists always befitted the characters involved; various escapades or heroics in which the characters indulged were the direct result of their personalities. All, therefore, was in order. The finesse and sensitivity the post-Realists brought to their art, the depth of their psychological analyses, the humor with which they garnished each of the episodes, added to the reader's involvement, moving him to tears or to laughter or to whatever mood the writer sought to project onto those who entered into complicity with him.

Duhamel began the cycle of the Pasquier family in 1933 and terminated it, ten volumes later, in 1944. Though he invented nothing new in terms of structure, his work remains fascinating because he succeeded in enticing his readers into the heart of a bourgeois milieu. There, he permits each of the individuals to burgeon forth, to develop, and at the same time to beguile or anger the reader who is forever responding to the various acts, ideas, longings, and quixotic antics presented him. With extreme simplicity and dexterity, Duhamel depicts the workings, both psychological and intellectual, of each member of the Pasquier family. These characters are never static, but rather evolve as they normally would in the workaday world—positively or negatively. Duhamel does not describe a character just once and then permit him to vanish. Rather, he proceeds in an impressionistic manner. Each time the reader confronts a certain personality, the descriptions are slightly altered, depending upon who views the protagonists, as well as upon the action involved. In this manner Duhamel succeeds in creating a feeling of fleeting time, of life as in a state of flux.

Duhamel ushers his reader into an everyday world, in which *feelings* are uppermost. Though the author is the supreme manipulator of his characters, they seem to move according to their own dictates. Duhamel never compels them into one path or forces them to adopt a certain and intransigent point of view. On the contrary, one feels that they are free individuals in their own right, that the author experiences their pathos, anguish, anger, moods of all types. Their daily life, therefore, becomes accessible to the reader through a variety of techniques adopted by the author: portraits, analyses, dialogues, descriptions, and narrative devices. Scenes are frequently described in order to lure the reader into a state of direct participation. He then considers the event in question, in terms of his own world; the characters' *presence,* both visual and psychological, conveys within him the impression of actuality.

I The Notary from Le Havre

The Notary from Le Havre (Le Notaire du Havre) (1933) is set in Paris in the year 1881. Raymond Pasquier, the father of four, though past forty years of age, decides to study medicine. His wife, Lucie Delahaie, is portrayed as a gentle, kind, and self-effacing mother who tends to her children, Joseph, Laurent, Ferdinand, and Cécile, with utmost love and gentleness. She works terribly hard completing her household chores, and, since her husband gives her little money, she is forever trying to make a little go a long way. One day Madame Pasquier receives a letter from the Notary at Le Havre, informing her that her half-sisters in Peru have made her the beneficiary of their will. The novel, in the main, consists of waiting for this inheritance, the legal complications involved and the anxieties aroused. Without his wife's knowledge, Raymond Pasquier, impulsive, impractical and self-centered, borrows money from a neighbor for investment purposes, offering him an inordinately high rate of interest. The investment proves to be a poor one, and the funds are lost. When the legacy does finally arrive, much of it is spent in paying the debts incurred. In addition to this central plot, there are interesting portraits, notably of the Wasselin family, neighbors across the floor: the mother, weak and ignorant; the father, a dishonest individual who is forever beating his son Désiré, making him feel utterly unwanted, and is instrumental in leading to his suicide at the end.

The Notary from Le Havre is a tightly woven work. Every aspect of this novel—from the fleeting descriptions of friends and neighbors to the family scenes, from the outer world of matter to the inner realm of feeling, from the rueful to the hilarious situations—is dexterously connected to the body of the saga. There is not one extraneous element to mar the general pattern drawn by the author.

Two main characters stand out most forcefully: Father Raymond Pasquier and his wife, Lucie. In order to introduce them to the reader most effectively as well as very dramatically, Duhamel begins his novel with a family scene. Like a Greuze portrait drawn in mellow tints, with great tenderness, all is there for one to perceive. The various trials and tribulations which beset the family are set in the dark shadowy areas: the sore and dismal aspects of married life, the difficulties involved when a husband is a flamboyant prima donna type as is Raymond Pasquier. Centrally drawn and in full light are the fears and courageous attitudes which Madame Pasquier experiences in turn as she encounters her daily existence, yielding always to her husband's choleric ways.

The atmosphere and the characters are masterfully delineated, both physically and psychologically. The aroma emanating from the slowly cooking lentil soup permeates the entire apartment each evening, inspiring those involved with a comfortable and secure feeling. Madame Pasquier is described as small, a bit stout, and wearing a chignon. Active in all of her undertakings, she is either sewing, cleaning, or cooking throughout the novel. Perhaps her most significant quality is what she comes to represent—the *ideal* mother, gentle, comforting, understanding, and, above all, loving. She is the epitome of strength, the guiding force behind her family. When, for example, one of her brood falls ill, as is a natural occurrence, she cares for him or her with solicitude, with efficiency, and always with calm. Madame Pasquier is also endowed with great feelings of consideration. When her husband is studying, for example, she makes certain the children are kept well away so that he can enjoy calm and peace. Madame Pasquier is not one to sit by and watch life pass by. Rather, she participates in all phases of existence through her family and in this manner experiences it deeply. In a way, she could be considered a sacrificial type, one who seeks to help others—forever and always—never once thinking of her own development as an individual. Indeed, she has no life whatsoever outside her family.

Raymond Pasquier who has just begun to study medicine as the volume starts, is an egocentric individual. He exists first and foremost for himself; his family is incidental. He is depicted by Duhamel as resembling the Frankish king, Clovis, because of his long moustache, his handsome and forceful face, his domineering ways. Everything is subservient to his needs, to his moods, and everyone bends instinctively to his will. Moreover, he is a person who unfortunately is unaware of his own limitations. He is convinced he is endowed with great business acumen and for this reason makes enormous mistakes in the world of finance. Nor is he easy to live with; irascible, quixotic, and given to frequent bouts of temper, life knows no calm when he is around. He is forever lending excitement to the saga. Because of his flamboyant ways, Raymond Pasquier has no friends. He is, furthermore, a man who suffers deeply because he is aware of the differences which exist between his aspirations—the ideals he has set for himself—and the reality of his situation.

Though there is a plethora of memorable characters in this novel, one person stands out above all: Désiré Wasselin. Duhamel's portrait of this young lad is masterful. He is ungainly, thin, and overly tall for his years; in this latter respect reminiscent of Flaubert's portrait of Charles Bovary. Fear is always engraved in his expression. The victim of an irrational father who is forever beating him while telling him he is unwanted and unloved, of a flabby-featured mother—one understands readily why he so desperately suffers from feelings of rejection. Moreover, the shame he knows as the offspring of two such unpleasant people is obvious in each of his words, in his glance, in his stooped shoulders, in his relationship with others. Rather than exteriorize the pain he feels at his father's rebuffs and castigations, at his mother's weaknesses, he hides it, experiencing it inwardly until the suffering has corroded his very being. When Laurent shows him kindness, he very nearly overresponds with an outpouring of warmth accompanied by extreme timidity. He has never been exposed to such feelings of gentleness before, and does not know how to react to them. The crushing finale to his wasted life is, of course, his suicide.

Each of the Pasquier children is described briefly and precisely. The reader, therefore, is aware to a great extent of how the budding traits, with which the children are endowed, may later develop. Since Laurent is the narrator in this saga, the protagonists are all seen through his eyes, in an understanding, kindly, and sincere way. The love Laurent bears his mother as opposed to the bitterness, anger, and near hatred he feels for his father is cogently expressed by means of dialogue and family portraits. Ferdinand is depicted as a hard worker but endowed with little ability or intelligence. Joseph, whom Laurent dislikes, is mercenary and rapacious. Cécile, already drawn to the piano, is still very young and, like an angel, comes to represent beauty and purity.

Duhamel is a master at creating suspense from seemingly routine episodes. The outside force--the Notary's handling of the aunt's will—acts as a catalyst, propelling the novel along and intruding upon the family situation in the form of news from the Notary or the lack of it or Madame Pasquier's visit to him. As time passes, the Notary's letter takes on even greater symbolic stature. Everything the family does or says now seems determined by the Notary's attitude. Though he is never there in person, his presence hovers over the entire family as would some impersonal god or regulator of destinies. The Notary in effect becomes the *deus ex machina* of this novel, bringing the family's emotional and economic situation to a climax.

There is another important protagonist in this novel: the city of Paris. Duhamel had brought this city to life in the Salavin series, thereby forming an important nucleus for the novel. He does likewise for the Pasquier works. The city thus becomes an intrinsic part of the Pasquiers' daily existence. The tortuous streets and avenues with their particularly pungent odors take on a life of their own as do the dismal parks and their shabby trees and stunted bushes. The various domiciles of the Pasquiers' also emerge as living beings—the Impasse Vandame, for example, with its lower bourgeois families, and the many abodes into which they are forever moving, both comfortable and distressingly small, sunny and dismal. Paris, as described by Duhamel, imposes itself in an utterly human manner upon the reader.

II The Garden of the Savage Beasts

Laurent is fourteen years old when the action unfolds in *The Garden of the Savage Beasts (Le Jardin des bêtes sauvages)* (1934). He is experiencing a period of discovery; he is just now beginning to see beyond the routine of his limited realm. The world outside of his family is taking on color and life. It is becoming both an enchanting and painful experience, but worthy of being confronted.

The title *The Garden of the Savage Beasts* is derived from Le Jardin des Plantes, where the Pasquier children used to spend so many happy hours at play. The focal point around which this second volume centers is Laurent's slow and painful discovery of his father's secret love life, his sordid liaison with a cheap-looking mistress, Solange Meesmacker. The naive and honorable Laurent is not only disconsolate but angered with the man he has always thought of as the leading and all-powerful figure in his world. He decides to take matters into his own hands. He goes to see Solange in order to break up the affair. He fails in this endeavor. When he confides in Joseph, he is further annoyed by his brother's matter-of-fact acceptance of the situation. Laurent is equally disturbed by his mother's reaction: she accepts reality though it is painful to her. She tries to explain her reasons for doing so to her son and in the simplest words possible. Morality, she says, has nothing to do with the admiration and respect the family bears Monsieur Pasquier; nor is it connected in any way with their love for him; the bad things in life must be accepted along with the good.

The rest of the Pasquier clan also develops. Ferdinand, myopic and introverted, lives in a world all his own. Cécile, the angel, spends her time practicing the piano and emerges more beautiful than ever. Joseph, the more materialistic member of the family, is forever downgraded by Laurent. Suzanne, the latest addition, is still tiny.

The Garden of the Savage Beasts is primarily a drama of adolescence. It describes the pain a young lad experiences when first confronted with the world about him, when just emerging from the protective realm of innocence and childhood into the *imprévu* world at large, filled with ugliness and terror. "The world order was imperiled and my position in the heart of this world, perturbed; it seemed rather frightening."[1]

Laurent, as a child, had always considered the world in terms of absolutes: good and evil. His family was all good and, since he had no real notion of evil, it was something relegated to some distant world of fairy tales. Evil had, therefore, left him untouched. This is not to imply that his realm was free from anxiety. He had experienced such feelings frequently, most particularly when he saw his mother in financial or emotional distress, when he watched her sew at night until the late hours, in order to pay for a pair of shoes for one of the children. He could cope with this kind of fear because he knew it so well. When, however, he discovers his father has other loves, other affiliations—that his family is no longer the solid unit he had once considered it to be—his world seems suddenly to crash. He experiences trauma, a hurt which will never really heal, at least not for many years to come. The greater the rage which centers about his father, the more deeply he feels linked to his mother. For this reason, he decides to assume the father's role in the house, symbolically speaking, to protect his brothers and sisters and most particularly his mother, from any pain his father might inflict upon them.

Laurent's visit to Solange is indeed an act of great courage. When he fails in his mission, he cannot help but look upon his father with growing distaste and disgust. Suddenly, he becomes aware that this man's strength, his domineering attitude, his inexplicable angers cannot really reach him. He loses his respect for Monsieur Pasquier completely. Indeed, he frequently considers him as a stranger: "My father's anger turns around us like a savage beast who is hunting." Their relationship becomes rather complex, particularly during Laurent's pubescence. He feels an extreme embarrassment at the thought of the sexuality involved in his father's existence. Sensitive and frustrated, he looks at him with ambivalent notions at times: with hatred for his immorality, with respect and love for his intelligence and for this dashing figure who is, after all is said and done, his father. The reader is imbued with Laurent's growing conflict: his impatience with Monsieur Pasquier's selfish ways, his deepening feelings for his mother who is the innocent victim of one man's caprices.

Laurent's hatred for his father reaches a climax in an absolutely unforgettable scene: Raymond Pasquier strikes his wife because she is unable to find his mistress's letter. Laurent is present at this hideous encounter, and when he sees his mother put her hand up to her face to shield it, in the manner of a child, and actually cower before such an ignominious person as his father, his heart beats with anger. Like his mother, however, he does not cry out. Rather, he suffers in silence as does a stoic.

The scene of confrontation between Laurent and Raymond Pasquier is also poignant and, in many ways, lugubrious. Laurent asks his father to renounce his mistress. Raymond Pasquier is annoyed by his son's daring to venture so overtly into his private territory; indeed, he ridicules his offspring for his naiveté. He then proceeds logically, at least from the point of view of his own rationale, and asks his son to compare his actions to those of other fathers. They are hypocritical, he states, whereas he, Raymond Pasquier, is sincere. His actions, he further declares emphatically, do not in any way detract from the feelings he has for his wife, his admiration of her goodness, and the beauty of her soul. Nevertheless, he too is endowed with personality, with fire and virility, and he does not want to stifle this aspect of himself because of family ties.

One has the distinct impression that Laurent, now aware of the situation, will try to accept it. He will no longer struggle to transform his father into the image of the ideal figure he had once nourished as a child. He will seek to accept him as he is and hide his feelings of rage, for the sake of peace and quiet. His pain will be turned inward for now. Moreover, Laurent is also in the process of discovering his own nature. He is sentimental and easily hurt, he realizes. He is not one of those beings endowed with a tough carapace, who can stand great emotional upheavals as a matter of course.

One outside figure imposes itself upon the Pasquier clan, Laurent's school chum, Justin Weill. He is and will remain, as the series progresses, one of the most fascinating characters introduced into the Pasquier home. Justin is a Jew who is not only unafraid of being a member of one of the oldest peoples but who is proud of his lot on earth. This is not to say that his world is not devoid of problems. He has many. He has been the victim of anti-Semitic remarks; he has overheard people cry out, "You dirty Jew," when referring to him or to members of his religious group. He is disconcerted frequently by some Jews who intermarry, giving up their birthright. Indeed, some even forget, neglect, or reject their heritage. They then begin to vilify other Jews in order to let the world know that they are "above" the group they have renounced and are now part of the majority. They feel contempt for their former associations and ancestors. Justin is ashamed of this kind of Jew. He discusses his ideas openly with Laurent—the differences, for example, which separate Christian and Jew, most particularly the question of the Messiah. For the Christian, the Messiah has already appeared; for the Jew he has not yet come. Other questions concerning Justin's ideals in life are broached in highly interesting discussions, such as his desire to be a famous Jew, thus bringing honor to his people. Duhamel's profound understanding of the Jew, of his beliefs, his feelings, and his sense of despondency when faced with mass extermination and persecution encountered throughout history, are quite uncanny. Moreover, Duhamel's respect for the Jews—their capacity for work despite unbelievable odds—comes through most excitingly.

When Justin falls in love with Laurent's sister, Cécile, the reader feels most acutely the young lad's awkwardness, not only because he is an adolescent—such problems always present difficulties—but particularly because he is a member of a minority people and fears, unconsciously, that he will be rejected. The Dreyfus case, with all of its ripples, was in ebullition at this period, and Jews, as a result, were most keenly experiencing the bitter hatred leveled against them.

Another character also emerges in this volume: Cécile's piano teacher, Valdemar Hemmingson, a Dane who has not succeeded in becoming a virtuoso and has, therefore, chosen the teaching profession instead. The description of his feverish playing, his loud and vociferous scoldings of his beloved Cécile, are beyond reproach. Duhamel's detailed account of Cécile's performance of a Mozart sonata is not only accurately transcribed, but the sensitivity and the impression the notes make upon Laurent as he listens is most unusually portrayed. All the senses, including the visual, are aroused. Duhamel infuses the reader with his own sentiments concerning music: that it is beyond description, that it nourishes and is a faithful companion at all moments of life, in joy as well as in sorrow.

One is always impressed in Duhamel's novels with his great feeling for nature in all of its phases. His finely etched portraits of clouds, as they move their massive hulks to and fro, of a solitary leaf, of the sounds emanating from foliage, from the onrush of water, those which cajole or jar the ear—all are imbued with depth and feeling. Indeed, the opening paragraph of *The Garden of the Savage Beasts,* a description of fish imprisoned in an aquarium, might accurately synthesize or symbolize everything that will transpire during the course of the novel. The Pasquiers are looked upon as a microcosm of the world, prisoners within its fold.

Exiled from native sands, captives in some glass aquarium, at the bottom of a laboratory . . . the small coastal animals continue, by means of a secret warning, to obey the rhythms of the tide, descending at flood-tide, rising when the ebb uncovers the distant coast.[2]

III A View of the Promised Land

The activities recounted in *A View of the Promised Land (Vue de la terre promise)* (1934) take place in 1900. Laurent is twenty years old and a scientist. Suzanne is eight; Ferdinand is an accountant; Cécile, a concert pianist; Joseph, a successful businessman; Raymond Pasquier has completed his medical studies and practices his profession at Créteil; Madame Pasquier becomes more and more of a sacrificial being. The inheritance due the Pasquier children has finally arrived. Joseph demands his share and a supplementary amount for having given up his studies, for having gone into the army, and for having been compelled to work at a very early age. When Laurent receives his thousand-franc note he decides to anger Joseph and, in so doing, express his contempt for him. He asks his brother to walk down to the river with him. There Laurent jumps on a parapet out of Joseph's reach and in a dramatic gesture throws his money into the water. Joseph, of course, is frantic. The rest of the novel narrates Laurent's unsuccessful attempt to confess his deed to a fellow scientist, Léon Schleiter, who is unwilling to listen, fearing that he might have to take sides in a family feud. Nor is the attractive Hélène Strohl ready to hear his story. Justin is the only one who lends an ear. He tells Laurent that his act was not really authentic since he had the thousand-franc note changed to two five-hundred-franc bills and only threw one away. Justin is dismayed by Laurent's lack of integrity; he tells him he should have discarded all the money.

We also learn that Cécile has fallen in love with her piano teacher Valdemar and intends to marry him. One day, however, Laurent sees Valdemar stealing morphine from his father's office. Now he understands why Valdemar has always been prone to fits of wild behavior. Laurent is determined to prevent his sister's marriage. Valdemar, unable to quench his need for morphine, shoots his mother and himself in a fit of despondency.

Other unpleasant incidents are narrated. Dr. Raymond Pasquier makes pregnant a poor relative, whom Madame Pasquier has taken into her home out of the goodness of her heart. Through a ruse, Laurent and his brothers succeed in getting this cousin out of the house, sending her back to the country from which she came. When their father discovers the treachery, he is not only angry but brings her back and, to add insult to injury, rents a small apartment for her near them at Créteil.

The final blow occurs when Laurent receives a letter from his friend Hélène Strohl, of whom he was fond, informing him of her engagement to Joseph. Laurent decides he can no longer bear his family life. He moves into a small apartment of his own.

A View of the Promised Land, as the title indicates, is centered around Laurent's glimpse of the promised land, that is, of independence and maturity. With infinite finesse, it recounts his inner struggles, his development, and his final break with his adolescent world and the subservient existence he has previously lived out vis-à-vis his family. At the outset of the novel, Laurent is still dependent, both financially and emotionally. His increasing contempt for his father prevents his attacking his own problem lucidly. He is ashamed of a man who cannot grow old gracefully and must forever feed his overbearing sensuality and ego at the expense of his family, a man whose flagrant disloyalty to his mother he considers unpardonable. Laurent, therefore, looks at the world in a negative manner. His feelings of hopelessness and desolation, when contemplating Madame Pasquier's fate, permeate his entire existence, his every act and thought. He is crushed by the pompous arrogance of his overbearing father, feels deeply for the sacrificial lamb who is his mother, who accepts whatever smile or affection her husband might cast her way. He cannot help but respond to the sadness which has engraved itself upon his mother's face, the depth of her silence, the genuine love she radiates about her.

Laurent's attitude toward his parents is in effect very negative: hatred for his father; extreme solicitude for his mother. He cannot develop under such circumstances, as is obvious when considering his rash act: casting his inheritance to the river. This rejection of the material aspect of life serves as the turning point in Laurent's psychological outlook. Aware of Joseph's utter possessiveness and his dependence upon money, he casts his bank note away primarily to enrage his brother, the one who had been so quick to accept his father's vagaries. Another aspect of Laurent's personality now comes to the fore. His flamboyant act gives him a feeling of superiority. It indicates his indifference to money. But is he really above the material aspects of life? Laurent has not sufficiently evolved to live out such an extreme point of view. He is a moderate always. The act itself is far too dramatic and not really in keeping with his personality. Had Laurent *really* overcome his need for the material, he would never have indulged in such an extreme gesture. To feel compelled to confess the truth about his act to others indicates his inability to falsify a situation, to live with a mask, and to abstract himself from his environment. It is only at the end of the novel, when he realizes the ludicrous nature of his gesture, that he comes to accept, at least intellectually, the fact that he cannot change others and that he had better concern himself with his own development—that his adolescence is very nearly coming to an end.

"I want to live, to live for me alone. I want to love. I want to enjoy the beauty of the world."[3] Had Laurent not opted for this new attitude, the walls of his world would have come tumbling down about him. He would have continued his shadow existence under his parents' wings, forever rebelling, living out a miasmic role in life. His reason is his guide, along with his feelings. Early in the first volume, we recognized that Laurent is a sensitive and understanding type. Moreover, he has a veritable lust for life. It is at this juncture, however, that he comes to realize that he must strike out on his own or forever be hurt. Life is to be lived in a positive manner, and each individual must carve out his own future alone. His gesture, though incomplete, since it had in part been false, indicates a desire for release and independence. Even if only on the unconscious level, he has already had a glimpse of that promised land. Now he will have to strive to reach it.

IV   Saint John's Eve

The fourth volume in this series, *Saint John's Eve (La Nuit de la Saint-Jean)* (1935), is narrated by Justin Weill. A victim of World War I, he has left a diary which his mother finds and sends on to Laurent. After certain changes, the manuscript is published.

The narration takes place in 1905. Laurent is twenty-five years old and is employed in both a hospital and a laboratory. Joseph, a wealthy and successful businessman, is the father of two sons. He has bought a large property which he calls La Paquellerie, and he lives on it like a medieval lord. He invites his family to celebrate Saint John's Eve. The party, however, ends unpleasantly. Professor Renaud Censier, Laurent's superior at the laboratory, a man for whom he has great admiration and affection, has been invited and, much to Laurent's distaste, expresses his inclinations for Laurent's friend Laure. Delcambre, an artist, indulges in rather off-color jokes and flirts with the thirteen-year-old Suzanne. As for Father Pasquier, he is as objectionable as ever. When Laurent finally returns to his apartment in Paris he finds it topsy-turvy. Much to his disgust, he discovers that his father has used his apartment for another one of his love affairs.

Saint John's Eve is probably the least interesting of the Pasquier series. There is little or no development of personality but rather a restatement of what we already know concerning the protagonists: Joseph's materialism—his need to display his wealth; Raymond Pasquier's being caught *flagrante delicto;* Madame Pasquier's continual suffering and her eternal attitude of understanding and forgiveness. The locale has changed, nothing more, save perhaps for the fact that Laurent has become more tolerant of his brother's ways. He begins to understand Joseph's veritable need for money, his feelings toward it—his belief that money is a creative agent. It is something to be used, something alive and capable of growth. Joseph explains his point of view:

Avaricious people are sick: I am sane like a new egg. I want money in order to create, I want money to be able to enjoy, because I love life. I too am a poet, I too am an artist . . . in my way. What is a creator? It is someone who makes something appear where there is nothing before. I am this kind of person![4]

With this added understanding of his brother's needs, Laurent no longer needs to be antagonistic toward him. His way of life of course will be different, but Laurent will no longer consider Joseph a threat to his well-being. He can, therefore, accept him as a human being rather than waste his energies in fruitless rejection of him, as he had in the previous volume, when he threw his money into the river. The Joseph type is one aspect of life, Laurent realizes, and must be coped with as such. Indeed, the Josephs of the world are necessary for society's survival and, therefore, have a positive function in life.

The remainder of the characters introduced in this volume seem contrived, as though especially invited to Joseph's home in order to hurt Laurent even further. None is sharply delineated nor sympathetic in any way. One can perhaps understand Laurent's deep admiration for his superior at the laboratory, Renaud Censier, but one fails to share this attitude because of the scientist's unpleasant manner and lack of integrity. As for the other fleeting beings who pass into Joseph's home, they seem utterly meaningless in thought as in deed. They are evanescent figures bearing merely names, appearing and disappearing without eliciting either thrills or sympathy. As for Doctor Pasquier, he becomes an even greater irritant. He is no longer interested in helping the sick but devotes his energies to women and inventions. In fact, he spends much of his money buying all sorts of patents which expire eventually and lead to numerous and complicated lawsuits. His actions, therefore, in all fields of endeavor, seem futile and irrational.

Only Justin Weill's personality is further developed in this volume. He tells of his trip to Palestine, of the emotions he experienced when witnessing the suffering Jews at the Wailing Wall. Though he had not been brought up in a religious household—in fact, had never really felt any affinity with his people—he is, nevertheless, deeply aware of his heritage. After his trip to the Holy Land, a new vision of his place in society comes to the fore: he experiences a most remarkable sense of relationship with other Jews in the world. In a poignant scene, Justin and Laurent are pictured riding in a Paris bus. A young lad with sideburns, an orthodox Jew, enters. Suddenly, inexplicably, a tidal wave of emotion wells up within Justin. He realizes at this second that the young man whom he does not know is in fact his brother, that blood and history link the two. The ability with which Duhamel captures this outpouring of feeling, which permeates Justin's being at this moment, is quite unusual.

When Laurent is finally alone, he seeks to assess his own life. He concludes that he is fighting a world which cannot be uprooted, which is unwilling and unable to change. His constant disillusionment, his inability to eradicate what is present, his negative attitude toward both father and brother, and his incapacity to come to terms with his own suffering trigger the pain which is to lead to his evolution. "I am too sad, too ashamed. I cannot explain this to you. And what is worse is that it's always the same thing. They won't change, neither the one nor the other."[5] Laurent is really ready to strike out on his own and to live positively.

V The Bièvres Desert

The Bièvres Desert (Le Désert de Bièvres) (1937) relates Laurent's experiences at a commercial undertaking outside Paris. The idealistic group, headed by Justin Weill with Laurent as his right-hand man, is motley: Bernard Jusserand and his wife; Jean-Paul Senac, an alcoholic who insults everyone; Testival, a bachelor and crank; Brenugat, a painter and his wife; Monmerque, the typographer who teaches the group the printing trade so that they can become self-sufficient as printers; Armand Larseneur, a pianist; and Madame Clovis, the housekeeper who steals the group's wine and is finally fired. Quarrels due to lack of funds and disparate and conflicting personalities serve to break up this once idyllic setup. No one is willing to assume responsibility; good will turns to anger. Justin's disillusionment is great, as is Laurent's.

Other episodes intrude. Dr. Pasquier, who takes fine care of Laurent during a serious illness, is pictured in another light. Moreover, he is the inventor of a new vaccine for which he is awarded the Legion of Honor.

There is no question but that *The Bièvres Desert* is to a great extent autobiographical, as are certain episodes of the previous volumes. This particular work reflects Duhamel's own experiences at the Abbaye de Créteil. Though written years after he himself had been part of an idealistic group of young poets, artists, and musicians bent upon changing the world, the fervor and the enchantment of youth, as well as its ensuing disenchantment are re-created with felicity.

In *The Bièvres Desert* we learn of the hardships which beset the young founders of the group. Because of their total idealism, they neglect something of extreme importance: coping with reality, the exigencies of daily life, the foibles and flaws in each human being's character. What youth lacks, of course, maturity possesses, and vice versa. When experience (the gift of maturity) can work together with fervor (youth's quality), then something stable and beautiful can emerge; when they work against each other, chaos can be expected.

The young men who found the Bièvres community do not have their feet firmly planted on the ground. Their lack of realism blinds them to the difficulties involved. They are living in an ivory-tower situation which engenders feelings of inflation within each of them, in various ways, protecting them in so doing, or veiling their sight. Their egotism, therefore, grows as do their innate cruelty and morbidity. They seek to gratify their own whims first—then those of others, if time permits.

The group decides in the very beginning that each will become an able printer in order to pay for the necessities of daily living. They will then be capable of printing the works of others. The rest of the time will be devoted to their own literary, artistic, or musical endeavors. Each is also bound to share in the physical labor required to keep the house and grounds clean. Like children, each of the lads trusts the others implicitly in the beginning, confiding in one another and looking upon the more mature members of the community as mentors. Yet, at the end, they come to realize that one cannot live in this kind of closely knit community without abdicating (or being willing to abdicate), at least to a certain degree, one's own personal desires, efforts, and freedom. Only in a monastic community, where faith is very nearly total, can such abandonment of self-interest occur. Neither Justin nor Laurent nor any of the others is sufficiently imbued with faith in his own goals to inspire it in others. The community cannot succeed. Sacrifice for an ideal is par for the course. These young lads are unwilling to give of themselves in order to shape their future along another course. So long as things go smoothly, both economically and esthetically, no conflict arises. The sham continues. However, once struggles occur, each in turn gives up the fight. Even Justin and Laurent finally realize that if they are to evolve as individuals they too will have to abandon the group which, to a certain extent, is stifling their development. Just as an adolescent must strike out on his own, must cut loose from family ties, so each individual in the Bièvres group has to cut his own river bed and build from there—alone.

It is Duhamel's extraordinary ability to re-create the excitement of youth—the ardor, the passion to succeed, even the disillusionment— which makes for the interest of this volume. With great tenderness, coupled with feelings of nostalgia and whimsy, Duhamel recounts the step-by-step change which each of the protagonists experiences. "We want to restore purity," they say. "Manual labor is in a way a type of sacred law."[6] The freshness and purity which these young lads seek is reminiscent in many respects of Rousseau's *La Nouvelle Héloïse* and Goethe's *Werther*, in which the healthy outdoor life, with its natural beauties, was re-created.

VI The Masters

The Masters (Les maîtres) (1937), in epistolary form, consists of letters from Laurent, who is working in a laboratory, to Justin, who is employed in a factory outside of Paris. Laurent describes his work, his feelings of admiration for his superiors: Nicolas Rohner, the cerebral scientist; and Olivier Chalgrin, who feels deeply about humanity. After Rohner dissects the body of Catherine Houdoire, his assistant at the laboratory, shortly after her demise from a disease contracted while studying certain cases, Laurent is thoroughly disgusted. In fact, he reacts violently to Rohner's callousness, his heartlessness vis-à-vis another human being. To make matters even worse, Rohner distorts his findings so that they will not differ from his theories concerning the cause of death. Laurent now speaks up. A quarrel ensues. Chalgrin is so shocked by Rohner's ruthlessness that he suffers a stroke and dies.

The novel's main theme is the portrayal of the dichotomy existing between two types of individuals: the cold, rational and objective scientist who thinks only in terms of his work and not the people involved; and the other type, which includes objective but tender and understanding workers who are involved in humanity's problems.

Duhamel attempts and succeeds in examining both types of men, who exist not only in scientific groups but in all walks of life. In the outset of the novel, Duhamel tries to explain the reason for the nationalist's point of view: "How would one not be rationalistic? The men of my age were nourished on this bitter and nutritive milk."[7] To have been taught that the mind is the highest aspect of man, that reason could and should never be dethroned, is to negate the whole affective world of emotions and senses—all those qualities and feelings which relate man to man. Man is not and cannot function in splendid isolation: he is part of a larger community and must, though perhaps not fully, participate in its development. Such involvement occurs both intellectually and emotionally, not one without the other.

Duhamel's description of Chalgrin, the scientist who experiences great feelings for others, who is endowed with extreme understanding, is sharply delineated. Chalgrin does not survive, because he takes the foibles of his co-workers too deeply to heart. He lacks callousness, an essential trait if one is to succeed in the world. He therefore represents the other extreme: the hypersensitive, the overly involved, the overly compassionate.

Laurent, the most arresting of the protagonists, tries valiantly to adopt a middle-of-the-road attitude as he makes his way, with difficulty, through the maze which is his life at this juncture. Each of the points of view is analyzed and dramatized through his eyes. In his assessment of both men, he is working out a formula for his own future. The experience of witnessing his colleague's death works on him deeply and, because pain churns within him, he begins to carve out his own vision of the world, gaining strength in so doing, so that he may become a fulfilled being in the course of time. The courage he displays when he speaks out forcefully against a superior in a laboratory is the result of his own meditations, his struggle with himself, his coming to terms with the reality of life versus his idealism. Laurent, in the future will not try to emulate Rohner, the cold and calculating individual, nor will he permit himself to be invaded by gushing feelings of shock, as experienced by Chalgrin. These also serve to crush *élan*. Each individual, he reasons, must have a firm base, learn how to experience solitude positively and build from there. No one should be so weakly structured as to be swayed by extremes. Laurent's new attitude precludes hero worship; all overt admiration for mortals and their capacity to create is now banished from this world. Slowly, he progresses to a state of maturity. He has confronted and come into conflict with certain dangers in life—in terms of personality types—and is now well equipped to assess them, to assimilate what is of importance to him, and to forge ahead for himself.

VII   Cécile Among Us

Cécile Among Us (Cécile parmi nous) (1938) concentrates on Cécile's unfortunate marriage to the dry and self-centered Richard Fauvert. Because Cécile is not happy with her husband, she concentrates all of her love on her son, Alexandre, and on her piano playing. Richard, aware and ashamed of the fact that he is unable to inspire feelings of warmth and love in his wife, devotes his time to literary endeavors. As the head of a literary group, he is burdened with the same problems which confront him in his marriage. He is a cold and sterile being, never inspiring any kind of affection in anyone. The more deeply he feels his deficiency, the greater is his desire to hurt his wife, to take his feelings out on her. She parries his attempts, save on one occasion, during a concert, when he flirts with her sister Suzanne. The wound is deep. The climax occurs, however, when Alexandre dies of a misdiagnosed appendicitis. There is now no longer any reason for them to stay together. Cécile goes to a convent for several months to try to recover from her excruciating grief.

The Pasquier family is again included, but only peripherally. Joseph indulges in a financial scheme, selling arms to both belligerents in the Bulgarian-Turkish war. Doctor Pasquier still looks upon himself as a young bull or Don Juan as far as women are concerned; moreover, he abandons medicine for a literary career and becomes the author of cheap novels. Ferdinand is more hypochondriacal than ever. Mother Pasquier, gentle and kind, is still intent upon keeping peace within the family.

The most touching aspect of this novel is Cécile's love for her son. The child is the center of her world; all else radiates outward. Indeed, the entire volume is constructed in the manner of a Racinian tragedy: the beginning and end are similar, touching upon the mother's feelings toward her son in life as in death.

This child— "this precious bundle whom she did not want to abandon, on this night, to anyone else"[8] —is her creation, and he brings her the most intense of all joys, the most exalting and noble of experiences. Duhamel brings understanding and depth to the various episodes dealing with the mother and son: from those instances of utter relaxation when Cécile gently hums to the child before he goes off to sleep, when he responds with joy in all-giving embrace, to the time when, desperately ill, he tries to reassure his mother of his well-being. The harrowing experience of the child's death is that much more cruel when juxtaposed to the beauty of the mother-son relationship. To withdraw this life is to kill the mother.

Laurent has become Cécile's main support. Reliable, kind, gentle, the brother who is always there, the scientist who can examine with lucidity and also with great understanding, he comforts her in her hour of need. Laurent stands out in this volume as an extraordinary human being in all respects. Mature, having himself struggled to evolve, he has become a composite of all the wonderful traits with which a doctor and a humanitarian should be endowed. Laurent is the type of person created for the purpose of helping others but never to the detriment of his own world or his own creative abilities: "It is not joy which fills the infinite spaces, the eternal silence, of which Blaise Pascal speaks. No, no, the world is filled with pain which cries out, which asks, throughout the centuries for justice and reparation."[9] Laurent has finally found himself; he is able to cope with the world and its problems on solid and effective grounds.

Fauvert turns out to be the villain of this saga. Cold, cerebral, and uncreative—in some respects similar to Rohner in the preceding volume—his brilliance, his philosophical and scientific acumen is to no avail. When he becomes aware of the terrible reality of his own emptiness, of the superficiality and aridity of his inner world—when he finally confronts the fact that he is nothing but a dilettante—he refuses to accept this reality. He fights it, blaming others for his own shortcomings. He is frightened, scared to death. Like an animal, he bares his fangs and tries to hurt the one person with whom he could have been happy—his wife. Jealous of her talent, of her charisma, he seeks to destroy her. In this manner, he thinks, erroneously, he can make up for his own inadequacies.

The musical interludes which Duhamel describes with such expertise are not set down on paper as images, as Marcel Proust described them in *Swann's Way*. For Duhamel, music is such an intense experience, such an integral part of his being, that he translates or transposes the effect of these tonal modulations in terms of his own senses and ideas: the notes caress his soul; they gnaw at his vitals; they soothe or arouse him as the case may be; they inflame or bring forth feelings of pathos, despondency—even anger. It is through music that both Duhamel and his characters, Laurent most particularly in this volume, are transported into another world, a realm of infinite beauty—and also sorrow. The manner in which Duhamel recounts the transition from the musical note to the emotion is valuable and meaningful.

VIII The Struggle Against Shadows

The Struggle Against Shadows (Le Combat contre les ombres) (1939) takes place in 1914, just before the outbreak of World War I. Laurent is thirty-three years old, works at the Pasteur Institute and is again confronted with moral problems. Lerminat, the head of the laboratory and an appointee who knows little concerning science, has chosen an inept researcher, Hippolyte Birault, to help in the laboratory. Laurent, who finds Birault totally inadequate—indeed, he very nearly ruins certain experiments—dismisses him. Lerminat, however, reinstates him. Laurent, infuriated by this lack of integrity on his chief's part, accepts the suggestion of a fellow scientist, Vuillaume, to bring the battle out into the open. Laurent writes newspaper articles concerning the political manipulations which go on in the laboratories. As time passes, Laurent realizes that his former friends are either too weak to side with him and confront the majority, or they remain uninvolved. Laurent resigns his post. The final blow occurs when Vuillaume is offered Laurent's position. He will accept it only if he can vindicate Laurent's name. World War I breaks out, and Laurent joins the armed forces. He therefore gives up one struggle to face another.

Plot ramifications are also part of this novel. Raymond Pasquier is still indulging in extramarital affairs and has become a charlatan psychologist as well. Cécile divorces her husband and slowly returns to herself. Laurent meets Jacqueline Bellac, a social worker, whom he marries.

The Struggle Against Shadows takes us into a world thoroughly familiar to Duhamel: that of the laboratory. In this instance, he takes an intransigent attitude and speaks forth clearly through Laurent. Scientists devoted to their professions, he maintains, should not become involved with any political group. Their lives should be devoted to science. There is no room in any laboratory for a political appointee interested merely in self-aggrandizement, in ego-building. The researcher's task is to help humanity as a whole; he should, therefore, be above the petty concerns of routine living and move steadily toward the scientific goal he has set for himself. In a way, the laboratory in *The Struggle Against Shadows* is comparable to the community described in *The Bièvres Desert,* in which each individual is dedicated to some artistic endeavor. The outstanding difference, however, is that the material problems of those working in a laboratory are taken care of, whereas in *The Bièvres Desert* these arose to plague the group. The scientist is concerned with the application of methods and the work involved.

Just as Duhamel believed firmly in the separation of church and state, so he felt that government should not intrude in the domain of the scientist. His feelings concerning these questions were never to change.

IX Suzanne and the Young Men

Suzanne and the Young Men (Suzanne et les jeunes hommes) (1941), like *Saint John's Eve,* is one of the least interesting volumes in the series. It deals very nearly exclusively with Suzanne and her theatrical career. Somewhat like Laurent when he was an adolescent, Suzanne is also an idealist and works hard as a member of a small theatrical art theatre run by Eric Vidame. Instead of awarding her the female lead in *King Lear,* which she both seeks and deserves, he gives it to an unqualified actress, the mistress of the company's producer. Suzanne, angered and hurt, leaves the troupe. Vidame, accustomed to the passions of youth, predicts her return.

Suzanne accepts the invitation of a friend, Philippe Baudouin, to live with his family at Nesles, in the country. There, once again, an ideal family situation is set up. Jérome Baudouin, the father, a blind war veteran, kind and gentle, lives with his wife, five daughters, and three sons. Each child is an entity in his own right: a botanist, a sculptor, a fine housekeeper, and so on. All are endearing and virtuous beings. Suzanne spends two months in this idyllic world, walking down country lanes, picnicking, singing at amateur song fests, giving dramatic performances, and the like. The atmosphere is one of joy, harmony, and conviviality. Suzanne thrives on the love displayed by all. One day, however, a member of Vidame's troupe visits her and suggests she leave with them on a South American tour. She does, forty-eight hours later, much to the distress of the Baudouin sons, who seemingly are in love with her.

Though interesting in the main for broaching the problem of a girl in love with the theatre, there is remarkably little suspense in this novel. The characters are not drawn in depth, the action is repetitious and tedious. The idyllic situation depicted has already been created and more forcefully in *The Bièvres Desert.* At Nesles, a realm removed from the turmoil and turbulence of city life, one has the distinct impression that Duhamel himself is trying to escape from his workaday world—France was occupied by the Nazis when he wrote this volume— and was longing to return to the old way, the past. He looked back to the time of his youth with nostalgia, a period removed from persecution, where beauty reigned, at least in retrospect. It is more a subjective recounting of Duhamel's ideal than a well constructed novel.

X   Joseph's Pasquier's Passion

Joseph Pasquier's Passion (La Passion de Joseph Pasquier) (1944), the last of the Pasquier series, analyzes Joseph's world and his downfall. Intent upon becoming a member of the French Academy, he does everything to achieve his goal. Unfortunately for him, however, the well-laid plans of mice and men have a way of turning on the instigator of such ideals. Joseph is rich; he has a mistress and two sons. Slowly, however, his investments are lost, his mistress is unfaithful, his wife has made him cuckold; his younger son, whom he had always looked upon as effeminate because of his wish to become a painter, jumps out of a third-story window. The volume ends as Laurent, who comes to the boy's aid, cannot give Joseph a definite answer as to whether the lad will survive or not.

In this final volume of the Pasquiers, Duhamel is in the process of tying all the strings together. A sense of doom and futility reigns in the novel. Laurent stands out as the only one who has found true happiness in life and in his work. Joseph, who has spent his years amassing a fortune, gathers nothing more into his orbit than problems. He has no friends and is despised by his wife and sons. His first offspring, a businessman like himself, is selfish, ruthless, and cold. The second, who is gentle and tender, whose temperament is artistic, is rejected *in toto* by his father. As for his wife, though he inspired feelings of love in her at the outset of their marriage, these slowly vanished when she realized that the material world was all-important in her husband's life, not the realm of feeling. The radiance of his personality—or what she thought it to be—has disappeared amid the thousand-franc notes and the gold bullion.

Joseph's attitude toward his father, which has never altered from the very first moment he expressed himself on the subject, is interesting in that it gives a glimpse of his entire character. He never despises his father, as Laurent does, on grounds of immorality or because he hurt his mother, but because he fears that other people might think badly of him. His existence, therefore, rests upon appearances—sham—and is based on the need to be accepted and admired by others. Laurent, whose feelings for his father are based almost exclusively on his notions of good and evil, does, after Dr. Pasquier's death, finally come to terms with his image. Indeed, he even forgives his father for having hurt them so cruelly. Laurent bears no grudge toward this man, because he has found happiness and need not have recourse to a scapegoat to vent his feelings. He has come to terms with his father's image because he himself has become a fulfilled man.

Though Laurent Pasquier most resembles Duhamel in terms of personality and profession, it can also be said that the other characters are also reflections, to a smaller degree, certainly, of the author: Ferdinand, so hypochondriacal; Suzanne and her love for the theater;

Cécile and her passion for the piano; Dr. Pasquier's ebullience; Madame Pasquier's tenderness, spirit of humility and understanding, and even optimism in the face of adversity.

In a sense, however, certain characters are drawn from life. Dr. Pasquier it seems resembles Duhamel's father in many ways. Pierre-Emile Duhamel began studying medicine late in life and earned his degree only two years before his son. Furthermore, Duhamel's father was also irascible at times; he also had eyes that were constantly drawn toward attractive women. As for certain emphases in these volumes, such as the stress laid on the laboratory, on scientists, on the creation of the community group in *The Bièvres Desert*—all these were drawn from reality. The artist Duhamel had therefore taken what he thought might be appropriate from the workaday world and combined this material with his own imaginings—as had his much admired Balzac—then molded the work of art which came to be known as the Pasquier series.

Certainly the writing of these ten volumes was a fulfilling experience for Duhamel, perhaps even more satisfying than the Salavin group. With the latter, Duhamel's range had been sharply restricted: one main character, his foibles and development; a series of peripheral characters who appeared most frequently in one volume and disappeared as rapidly thereafter. The central anecdotes were also limited in scope, since Salavin's abilities were far from varied. The Pasquier volumes, on the contrary, take the reader into various métiers and trades, several strata of society, which are all described in detail, as is every member of the Pasquier family. Moreover, Duhamel introduces absolutely intriguing personages such as Justin Weill, Robert Fauvert, and others, who are drawn with depth and finesse. In this manner the author could better express his own ideas concerning science, politics, literature, the theater, music, and children.

Though Duhamel had his own social and moral code, the Pasquier series cannot really be looked upon as "thesis" novels. Quite true, Duhamel denigrated the materialism of anyone who, like Joseph, believed money to be the *sine qua non* of life; he believed fervently in honor and integrity as virtues capable of bringing one fulfillment and happiness; he was certain that love and kindness, man's most admirable gifts, should be central to one's relationships throughout life. Yet he did not fly the banner of the "thesis" novel as did Emile Zola and the Goncourt brothers. Duhamel's intention was limited in this respect to the creation of a family and the dramatization of its course through life, in the same manner, perhaps, as Roger Martin du Gard had done in *The Thibaults.*

One finishes the series with the feeling that the Pasquier's struggles are ours, that their way of dealing with iniquities can also be understood by us, that the task of living life thoroughly is indeed difficult, but worthy of the effort. When man is able to devote his energies to bettering the lot of his fellow beings, when he can enjoy balance and harmony within his own soul, he has come a long way. He then becomes the Laurent of his generation, as perhaps Duhamel was of his.

CHAPTER 7

Pacifism: Its Painful Repudiation

D UHAMEL HAD ALWAYS BEEN a pacifist by nature. He was also a patriot. With the advent of World War I, he realized the necessity for fighting. There was no choice. After the war, however, he advocated peace both verbally and actively. He had seen enough suffering in the trenches, sufficient agonies, too many young maimed.

After the signing of the Treaty of Versailles (June 28, 1919) Duhamel advocated a *rapprochement* with France's former enemy. He was convinced that by talking out problems, honestly and thoughtfully, future wars could be prevented. He therefore went to Germany after the "Great War" and spoke with university students, professors, writers, artists, and government officials, concerning future developments between European nations. He was sanguine. He had always made a sharp distinction between the "war-makers" and the German people; they should never be confused, he maintained. The people were the innocent victims of those who fought for aggrandizement, possessions, and power. The military men were the ones to be feared; they were always attempting dominion over neighboring countries in their quest for *Lebensraum.* Certainly, after World War I, he reasoned, they would be stopped; they had been defeated and could easily be kept in check.

With the advent of Hitler, however, in 1932, Duhamel's feelings concerning Germany began to alter. He saw Germany—its leaders only—for what it was: militaristic, aggressive, ruthless. The rise of the National Socialist party (Nazis) under the leadership of Adolf Hitler frightened him because the party had taken on such monstrous proportions and had gained such momentum. Because of Hitler's immense popularity, Germany's president, von Hindenburg, invited him to become chancellor. In 1933 a new election was then held and Hitler's party won a majority in the Reichstag. The Weimar Constitution was set aside and dictatorial powers were conferred upon Hitler.

Duhamel was deeply concerned. Yet he felt that peace could still be maintained, and he worked hard toward this end, writing articles, speaking fervently for the cause which he so long sought to have prevail.

The situation in Germany was growing steadily more frightening. The year 1934 was the year of the "blood purge." Most of Hitler's opponents were put to death. After von Hindenburg's demise (1934), Hitler was not to be stopped. As chancellor, he furthered the politics of the Nazis and created a powerful dictatorship. From 1935 to 1938, he added hot coals to the already tense situation. He was impregnating the entire continent with his insidious disease: conquest, purge, annihilation. Hitler first did away with the Versailles Treaty and increased his army to over one hundred thousand men (1935). He then disregarded the regulations set in the Locarno Treaty by marching his troops into the demilitarized Rhineland area (1936). Austria was seized in 1938. Czechoslovakia was dismembered. And the entire world watched!

Though the dream of peace still glowed in Duhamel's mind, he could not but sense the growing discontent in his own country. His anger grew at the thought of another conflagration. He tried, desperately, to understand Hitler's rationale. He soon concluded that no amount of reasoning or argumentation could conjure forth excuses for Hitler's actions. But he still maintained that distinguished Germans, though in the minority, lived and advocated that marvelous *Kultur* brought forth by the Beethovens, the Schumanns, the Goethes, the Heines, the Schopenhauers. The thinking men, though positive forces in Germany, could no longer be heard above the din of clashing armor and churning steel—marching men.

Hitler and his Nazi horde sought conquest and conquest alone. Any means was acceptable for accomplishing their ends. The concentration camps, the wholesale slaughtering of Jews set Duhamel into a state of despair. In *Defense of Letters (Défense des lettres)* (1937), a volume which consists of a series of essays and meditations, Duhamel, though speaking out against Hitler's methods and plans, still voiced his faith in the power of the printed word—the book—hoping beyond hope that reason would in some miraculous way prevail over passion.

Duhamel had always been convinced that the book was the true propagator of culture; it was one of the most powerful instruments for the distribution and diffusion of knowledge. What would happen, he questioned, should a new disease appear which would attack paper and reduce libraries to dust? Would men live in a state of ignorance? He was most certainly referring to his neighbor Germany, to the burning of books in the universities. He looked with dismay at this curtailment of intellectual freedom. It could only herald ominous consequences. Would the best of man be destroyed? Any system of government which seeks to curb man's creative powers (whether it be Stalinism in Russia or Hitlerism in Germany) inspired feelings of revulsion in Duhamel.

Duhamel could not accept the tenets of any government whose purpose and function were to destroy individualism. He had spoken forth for individual effort in all domains. The rulings of a central institution which advocated collectivity were therefore anathema to Duhamel. He looked with admiration at the government which encouraged individual creative effort, which not only permitted but advocated the reading of *all* books, with free discussions concerning them. Mass propaganda campaigns, presented to the people in the form of pictures, could stifle imagination and destroy initiative. Rather than taking the trouble of reading an article, Duhamel declared, people would become lazy and merely glance at photos printed all over a tabloid. They would believe anything and everything they saw since they would never bother reading the article alongside the picture or others which might be offered in disagreement of the view printed in the paper. Such a situation had already come to pass in France, Duhamel declared; culture was something which lived in the past.

Duhamel defined culture in the following manner. "Culture," he wrote, "is founded on the comprehension of phenomena of men and their works." Machines, movies, photographs, advertising campaigns impede the individual's ability to reflect, to ponder. Without thought, meditation, and solitude, masses can be swayed and swept off their feet in the most violent and vicious of ways.

When looking toward his own land, to French authors, Duhamel was dismayed to discover that most of them no longer strained and pained over their writing. Everything had become facile, simplified. Modern authors could not compare, in this view, with those of the past. Gone was the feeling of "religious ecstasy" which arose in the author when he confronted the blank page before him; forgotten was the sense of respect for the white page he was going to blacken with letters, for the instrument with which one labors for hours on end, trying to perfect what pours forth from man's innermost recesses. Today, Duhamel lamented, writers are like spoiled children. They are accustomed to facile success, to a lot of money, to blatant advertisements. He urged the youth of France to beware of the easy road, to be on constant guard against quick adulation.

Duhamel had voiced this concern in *Discourse to the Clouds (Discours aux nuages)* (1934). He advised modern writers to work on their style, to cultivate clarity and precision in their expressions, to render the ambiguous lucid. Repetitions should be avoided; they become tedious and indicate either a lack of thought or an inability to express it in succinct and meaningful terms. A writer, he further stated, should be many things—an artist, a confidant, a philosopher, a guide.

Nothing but talent and arduous labor can "manufacture" great writing. Neither drugs nor any artificial stimulant can bring forth the work of art. Extreme lucidity, perseverence, toil—these are the tools of the writer. Dazed and hazy thinking, muddled and confused means of expression have never brought forth anything but mediocre books. Man must work toward applying his reason, his spiritual insights, and put these to positive use. Feelings and emotions are not sufficient; they are energizers, catalyzers, but they must be articulated, structured and patterned into meaningful formulations.

Whenever Duhamel felt particularly distressed, as he did during the turbulent period when Germany was again becoming a threat to world peace, he always had recourse to music. Whether he played the flute or merely hummed the melodies he so loved, usually airs from Bach or Mozart, he derived solace and relaxation from them. He felt as though he were invaded by a type of inner peace, as though he had come into direct contact with his soul. When in such moods, his negativism began to vanish. Perspectives were no longer lost; ideals still seemed within the realm of possibility. Indeed, through music he seemed to gain greater lucidity in his attitudes toward certain situations, ways and means of coping with formerly insoluble matters. Music, therefore, was not only a source of joy, balance, and harmony—a particularly comforting experience—it also acted as a stimulant, inspiring him in his writing. Indeed, he frequently hummed tunes while writing, or when rereading what he had just set down on paper. "I can hum tunes if they happen to fit in with the rhythm of my thoughts," he wrote in *Defense of Letters.*[1] "I select these melodies instinctively and I abandon them when they are no longer in unison with my inner music." He felt that each style of writing possesses its own particular music. It is the artist's task to discover it, its particular phrasing and harmony. The musicality the writer senses in his work, the varied tonalities and rhythms he feels, lend depth to his writings. The clarity and moderation Duhamel experienced most forcefully in Bach and Mozart should, he declared, act as guidelines for the writer.

Duhamel still and always turned to nature as a source of joy and learning. In *Fables from My Garden (Fables de mon jardin)* (1936) he describes the flowers, shrubberies and animals which inhabit it. In veiled terms, he attacks society and its evils, its materialism, hypocrisy, the lack of effort displayed by its citizens, by finding analogies in the plant and animal world. An atmosphere of sorrow was passing over his garden, he declared, when he came to such conclusions. It looked deserted, he cried, and mournful; the leaves were immobile; "our trees no longer know how to sing, and flowers no longer tell their stories."[2] Pain over a growing feeling of imprisonment and constraint seemed to manifest itself in Duhamel's garden at this time. In a superb paragraph, he describes the encroachment of the primeval forest into the cultivated areas. The former represents the instinctual side of man, as exemplified by Hitler's Germany, the side which seeks to deal a death blow to rational forces; the latter symbolizes what man labels as "civilization." Duhamel concludes:

Each day the forest exercises its pressure on man's domain and makes an effort to invade it. The gardener, at each instant, pulls up a little oak, a clump of acacias, a hazel tree, which has slipped into the hedge, the prairies . . . and tried to grow there. When watching the garden fall into the hands of the terrorists, the forest begins its march. Slowly, but with invincible might, the forest would sweep away the agitators, the malcontents, the seasonal masters. At a future time, the garden would disappear in the murmuring shadows of the great, savage, fully grown trees. And our world would resemble its obscure beginning.[3]

The forest will not be the only entity to encroach upon the civilized world; cities will grow like giant cancers and expand, annihilating everything in their wake. In *At Civilization's Bedside (Au chevet de la civilisation)* (1938), Duhamel was convinced that Europe was going through not merely a political and economic crisis, but one in which civilization itself was at stake. Upheavals were in store for mankind. Because of modern man's overreliance upon industry, he predicted future traumas. Cities would be the most fitting examples of chaotic conditions initiated by such a turn of events. They have become unwieldly. Man has been severed from nature because of the industrial environment he has created. Yet, since he is part of nature he must of necessity follow its laws. If he does not, he will pay the penalty with his own destruction.

The megalopolis, a product of modern times, can create only disorder. Capitalism, which produced these large, anonymous, and unfriendly entities, will suffer its own undoing within them. Huge machines, tremendous cities, and dense populations will give rise to combustion, fire, and devastation.

Duhamel was convinced that a gigantic conflict would ensue. Such a state of affairs would not only come to pass because of man's inability to handle the machine and modern forces of destruction but because of the confrontation of ideologies at stake: good versus evil.

I *The Holocaust*

The holocaust was approaching. He voiced his fears in a short story, "Candide's Last Voyage" (1938). The tale concerns an old Candide who has spent his years cultivating his garden. Before dying he wants to see the outside world just once again. He leaves his own land and a guide shows him other countries which look so beautiful and orderly, so friendly on the outside. After further investigation, however, he learns that all those inhabiting these countries must agree with the ruling faction or be imprisoned. All vocal opposition is crushed. Candide, dismayed by such a lack of freedom, returns to his own little spot and decides to spend the remaining years of his life cultivating his little garden.

The greater the possibility of a conflagration, the more past memories kept emerging. It was as if Duhamel were reliving World War I, viewing the agony of the mutilated, responding to the longing glances of the dying. Though Duhamel had advocated friendship ever since the cessation of hostilities in 1918, he could no longer conceive of peace as an even remote possibility. The terror of the Teutons was again wreaking its havoc; the humiliations, not to speak of the cruelties and tortures, imposed upon others, could no longer be overlooked. "I have no more illusions," he wrote in *Fables from My Garden.*[4] The military had taken over.

In 1938 Germany was fully rearmed. She had become the foremost country in Europe. Her leadership and her strength were not to be denied. Duhamel realized that Hitler had fired the Germans with an ideal, had infused them with zeal and energy and was leading them toward a *Weltanschauung* based on world domination, hate, revenge, and racism. The Munich Conference (September 29, 1938) had marked Germany's official mastership in European affairs; she was now the one to dictate politics in Europe.

Duhamel was not overly shocked when Germany broke the Munich pledge, when she signed the Russo-German mutual assistance pact.

What made him rage, however, was the virulence of Hitler's anti-Semitic campaign, the concentration camps where mass exterminations were taking place. Goebbels' machine had extended its tentacles with the wildest fury and was annihilating with precision, alacrity, and deftness. What other disease—except for total destruction—marches with such totality, invades with such complete perfection. Coupled with Goebbels' and Hitler's hate campaign were the militarists in Berlin who, reiterating the teachings of Fichte, Hegel, and Treitschke, suggested that Germany launch a war of conquest for necessity's sake.

The Germans' hatred for France was another source of anguish for Duhamel. Now, the Germans stated unequivocally that France—their enemy—must be totally and completely annihilated. Heretofore, Duhamel had sought to distinguish between the "good" Germans (poets, musicians, painters, philosophers, scientists) and the aggressive, ruthless, destructive types. He had reached such an emotional pitch at this period, however, that he could and would no longer make the distinction.

He was incensed by Hitler's seizure of Czechoslovakia. He had always felt great warmth, a very special affinity, for the Czech people. He admired their ideals and declared, upon his very first visit, that he could actually "feel their soul." He admired their innate sense of freedom and righteousness, their courage and fierce loyalty to the principles of democracy. He had known Tomáš Masaryk and Eduard Beneš personally; their idealism and integrity had deeply impressed him.

Politically speaking, the loss of Czechoslovakia did not bode well for France. Bismark had once said, "Whoever is master of Bohemia is master of Europe." This statement was as true in the twentieth century as it had been in the nineteenth. Hitler had taken this land, using a feeble excuse to explain his deed. He demanded, he said, "self-determination" for the Sudeten Germans, the minority living in Czechoslovakia. When Hitler forced the annexation of the predominantly German-speaking area of Czechoslovakia at the Munich Conference, he was granted his wish by Neville Chamberlain, who furthered a policy of appeasement, and by Edouard Daladier and Georges Bonnet who seconded it. These men repudiated the French treaty calling on their country to defend Czechoslovakia in case of attack. Unaided, Czechoslovakia could do nothing but submit.

Munich, Duhamel wrote in *The White War (La Guerre blanche)* (1938), was not a peace treaty; it was "an armistice." In this slim volume, Duhamel collected a number of essays he had written between July and November, 1938. He stated that the Munich Pact had served merely one purpose: to suspend the march of the criminal Germans; it had not abolished it. When Hitler used the feeble excuse of the three and a half million Germans living in the Sudetenland who, he said, had been cut off from the *Vaterland,* Duhamel could not help but retort questioningly: what of the millions of people living in utter terror and oppression with Germany proper? No answer, of course, was forthcoming.

"The Big Four" (Hitler, Mussolini, Chamberlain, and Daladier) worked out the details for Czechoslovakia's dismemberment. On October 1, the Germans occupied the Sudetenland. By March, 1939, the rest of the country had fallen under Hitler's control (Bohemia, Moravia, Slovakia), and the dreadful tragedy of subjugation, suppression, destruction, and servitude began.

The surrender of countries like Czechoslovakia and Poland indicated Germany's intention of extracting the "marrow" from all conquered lands.[5] Hitler's party, Duhamel was convinced, would not collapse nor would it vanish. Steps would have to be taken to rout out the enemy by force. For a man who had always preached understanding and pacifism, to speak in such forceful and belligerent terms was fitting to the occasion, if not to the personality.

Duhamel compared Nazi Germany with Sparta; the rest of Europe, with Athens. The world could have lived without Sparta, he declared, but not without Athens. The talent and the intelligence of the people of Germany could have been used to manufacture books and music, art and philosophical works. Instead, the energy had been wasted on manufacturing armaments of destruction: airplanes, incendiary bombs, and so on. The flower of Germany's youth had been persuaded to destroy.

The real tragedy for France, Duhamel further remarked, was that she was unaware of the pitfalls which surrounded her. France would have to learn through pain and anguish to reinforce the law of the land. She would have to attempt to ward off destruction and conquest in whatever way she knew how. In describing man and his primeval and instinctual aspects, Duhamel again had recourse to nature. Just like certain plants, he wrote in *Why France Fights (Positions françaises)* (1940), each flower or shrub is endowed with a character of its own:

some are gluttonous and brutal, others are clever and tortuous, others patient and clinging. Certain have all these qualities at the same time.

They think only of spreading out, of ridding themselves of all neighboring spaces, in smothering and destroying the most delicate plants, which are always the most beautiful and the most necessary as well.[6]

Just as flowers must protect themselves from aggressive and poisonous relatives, by strengthening their foliage, their roots, so must man do likewise. No one more than Duhamel, at this juncture, realized the gravity of France's plight. The feelings of friendship, of hospitality, of forgiveness, of mutual encouragement had given way to notions of anger. The madness of Germany's expansion was disseminating its venom all over Europe. It had to be stopped.

Duhamel again reiterated his feelings concerning dictatorships in *Why France Fights*. A land where wiretapping takes place, where people are forever being interrogated and with the most bestial devices, where the giving of drugs is *de rigueur* whenever information is to be extracted from individuals, where torture, gas chambers and other horrendous acts are perpetrated without flinching an eye—such a land must not be permitted to dominate the world. Death, he declared, lurks in every corner of every street in Germany. To eliminate freedom is to kill outright. The time was ripe for war. France must—and now—face her enemy. He recalled, in this same volume, the time his father used to tell him about the war of 1870, when Germany first invaded France. His father had been mobilized on that occasion and had fought several battles, including Busenval and Champigny. One could not forget Germany's lust for power.

What Duhamel feared most strongly was about to take place. The Nazi troops crossed the Danish frontier and established themselves in Norway, the Netherlands, Belgium, and Luxembourg. Hitler, with over a million men, was ready to launch his attack on France. The Maginot Line was overrun and the Nazis crossed the Somme, the Aisne, and the Marne rivers. Paris was taken on June 14, 1940. Marshal Henri Pétain asked for an armistice. In a railroad car in the forest of Compiègne, the French signed the armistice treaty on June 21, 1940. This document left Paris and northern France in Germany's control. A government at Vichy, headed by Henri Pétain and Pierre Laval, was then established.

It was during this formidable time that Duhamel left Paris. From May to July, 1940, he worked as a physician in a converted convent, which, though far from the front lines, was still not far from German bombs. Once again he spent his days caring for and operating upon the wounded. This time, however, his patients were not only soldiers, but included civilian casualties caused from the continuous bombings. It was as if history were repeating itself, Duhamel remarked in the journal he kept at this period and which was later published under the title *A Place for Shelter (Lieu d'asile)* (1940). He worked long hours and once again had to harden himself to the cries of the suffering, to the wails of infants and women, struck by incendiary bombs on roads, in their houses, and elsewhere. He personally cared for from five hundred to six hundred casualties with the same devotion and solicitude he had in 1916. He described the cases he had seen, the mutilated soldiers, the mothers without legs, children, nurses, and old people, all maimed, bloodied—all those brought to him for one reason or another. Though the names were different, the pleading glances of the agonizing, the groans of the amputees, the lacerated, the eyeless, the frantic—it was as if a sequel had been written to *The New Book of Martyrs* and *Civilization.*

Despite the cruelties he saw perpetrated, Duhamel never despaired. It was not in his nature to indulge in negativism. He knew that one day peace would reign and that France would emerge victorious. The chaos that was being experienced in his land was temporary, one of the evils with which man must cope every now and then. To symbolize his feelings of optimism for the future, he had recourse to the image of a child born in the hospital in which he cared for the wounded. Everything this infant stands for, he wrote in *A Place for Shelter*—future, life, growth—all these things will come to pass. " 'A child was born!' He was born as the new France is going to be born, he was born from a wounded creature, broken, bloody, but still proud, still strong and resolved to triumph over misery."[7]

Though France had lost, Duhamel wrote, the soldier could be proud of the way he struggled to protect his land from the enemy. He was worthy of admiration. His forefathers had done their best to ward off the evils facing their country—and so had the fighting man in 1940. After France had capitulated and the French army was demobilized in 1940, Duhamel returned to his beloved city of Paris. There he remained for the duration of the war. He refused to leave, he wrote, for he wanted to experience the fate of his compatriots, the hardships they were to know, the turmoil and anguish.

A Place for Shelter was printed in 1940. When the Germans discovered the volume they had it burned. They told Duhamel, however, that if he would be willing to say something nice about them in his book, they would permit another printing. He refused, as was to be expected, and very few volumes escaped destruction. It was not reprinted until 1944.

II *The Occupation*

During the dismal years of the German occupation, Duhamel never gave up hope. In *French Civilization (Civilisation française)* (1944), he expressed his belief in the allied victory and felt convinced that France would once again assume her rightful place among world powers. France had always triumphed in the arts, sciences, literature, theater, and cuisine. It had been the land of humanism and the cradle of rationalism. Such a country, he wrote, always mistrusts excesses of any kind and, therefore, would be a primal force in creating a unified Europe after the holocaust.

Until peace was declared, however, until his dream of unified Europe might become a reality, Duhamel had to cope with the horrors of the occupation. In *Words of a Doctor (Paroles de médecin)* (1946), he gives his readers detailed accounts of the dismal conditions in the Parisian hospitals: the cold and dampness, the scarcity of personnel, the valiant search for technicians, the use of substitute materials to replace those which could no longer be acquired such as cotton, rubber, vaseline, and the like. Frequently, Duhamel wrote, the hospitals were so cold and the conditions so unsanitary that the patient did better to remain at home. In all of his writings of this period, Duhamel never forgot to talk of the doctors who fought in the resistance—those men he singled out for particular praise.

Duhamel was compelled to write in secret during the occupation. He published his works clandestinely and did his best to help the civilian resistance. It was during this period that he wrote *Chronicles of the Bitter Seasons 1940–1943 (Chroniques des saisons amères 1940–1943),* a volume of meditations and essays on the problems of civilization and occupation.

In the section of this volume devoted to the growth and development of civilization per se, Duhamel advocated once again the study of humanities and the teaching of Latin. Both of these subjects developed and trained the mind. They rendered it young and malleable, like a muscle. To teach humanities to the young is to permit them to develop finesse and an understanding of life in general. Other passages in this book were concerned with discussions he had had years before with André Gide about Dostoevsky, with Roger Martin du Gard, and with other creative artists. Essays on grammatical phrases, dictionaries, style, and self-discipline are also included in *Chronicles of the Bitter Seasons*. The elegy of the city of Paris is perhaps the most moving section in the entire work: it describes man's daily sacrifices in the face of the ruthless invader.

The tide was slowly turning. In 1944 one of Duhamel's friends, the writer Tristan Bernard, who had been imprisoned by the Germans and who had finally been released, said to him: "Until now we have lived in anguish. Now we will live in hope."[8] For four years the French had had to cope with the enemy in their midst, to submit to the ignominies of occupation. Duhamel expressed his anger in *Tribulations of Hope (Tribulations de l'espérance)* (1947). Gone was the reasonable attitude he had once maintained; gone were the abstract philosophical notions.

Tribulations of Hope is a type of diary which Duhamel kept, which he began in August, 1944, shortly before the liberation of Paris, and continued until December, 1946. In this volume, he salutes the Dutch and the Belgian soldiers—all European soldiers who had helped crush the enemy. He believed in their sacrifices now, in their martyrdom—and most fervently. He hoped—and strongly—that the guilty would be punished, that they would serve as examples for future generations, that such excruciating behavior would not be permitted to occur again.

Other questions were also treated in this volume. As permanent secretary to the French Academy, Duhamel was preoccupied, in 1942, with the problems of printing. Very little paper was available, and still less was being manufactured. The question arose as to whether the limited amount of paper should be used to print new books or to reprint classics. Duhamel's son, who was studying for his doctorate at the Sorbonne at the time, could not avail himself of any of the books he needed. His father and he combed the bookstores of Paris. No results. It was as if these books had been completely destroyed. Duhamel, therefore, urged that the classics be reprinted. France's greatness, he wrote, resides in her literature.

The classics had always fascinated Duhamel. In *Confessions without Penitence (Les Confessions sans pénitence)* (1941), a volume of essays devoted to Rousseau, Pascal, Montesquieu, and Descartes, he evaluates the contributions of these men. After a brief biographical statement, he analyzes some of their literary works and their most outstanding personality traits. Concerning Rousseau, he declared that one would have to be pure spirit to consider him and his work objectively. Yet, despite the fact that Rousseau was a complex of faults—the worst of which were his lack of self-discipline and his abandonment of his five children—his prose is extraordinary and French letters owe him a great deal. Perhaps what Duhamel responded to most of all in Rousseau was his incomparable artistic sense, the fact that by means of his style he was able to beguile people—even their souls. Duhamel was fascinated by Montesquieu's brilliant and agile mind and by his predictions as well. Indeed, it was Montesquieu who, in the eighteenth century, predicted a gas war. As for Descartes, Duhamel felt that he was overly rational, that he had not developed any regard for other sides of man's personality: his senses, his heart. Pascal, one of Duhamel's favorites, was a man forever struggling to reconcile faith and reason. He had always maintained that pride was one of the greatest obstacles to faith. Duhamel, however, felt that "honesty" was a deterrent to belief in church dogma. When man does not have faith, Duhamel declared, it would be dishonest of him to claim himself a believer. Duhamel, who had lost his faith early in life, who was still agnostic and who still believed in honesty, had no patience at all with the hypocrite. He could not, despite Pascal's wager, maintain any other attitude toward salvation.

III *Liberation*

When the liberation became a reality and Duhamel saw the much-hated enemy depart, he was infused with a sense of extreme joy. Despite the impoverished land, the destitution, the loss to life and limb, the sense of release and giddiness he now knew, compelled him to walk the streets of Paris in reckless exhilaration. He wandered through the avenues, the small winding alleys, everywhere and anywhere, savoring this "miraculous moment" to the extreme. It was as if Paris—France—breathed anew.

Duhamel was certainly not oblivious to the fact that the road ahead would be difficult, that extreme energy and effort would be needed to rebuild the land, to imbue the people with the pride shorn from them during their years of defeat. Duhamel could not, at least for the moment, feel "charity" toward his enemy—that feeling François Mauriac had advocated so freely. Duhamel was adamant now. The guilty parties must be punished; the traitors, chastised.

The Nuremberg trials began. Time was passing, and Duhamel became more and more annoyed by the procrastinating Americans. He knew—and they knew—who the guilty ones were. There were no excuses to be made. Unless the guilty were punished and a strong regulating force established, Duhamel wrote, a third world war would be in the offing. This time, however, England would play the same role Belgium had played in 1914 and France in 1940. America would remain alone—isolated in her splendor—to face the enemy.

When the atomic bomb was dropped on Hiroshima, Duhamel felt that this weapon had not really served to crush the enemy. The war had ended before this horrendous event. Furthermore, he predicted, in ten years, most countries would have the atomic bomb. Secrecy concerning this weapon would be impossible. People, in their desire to possess destructive armaments, would never be willing to limit their hoard of nuclear weapons. Specialists were already at work building up more and more destructive weaponry. One day, Duhamel predicted, atomic conflict would take place and with no declarations of hostilities. Vital services in nations would be involved and destroyed. Explosions would devastate the land. This surely would be the war to end wars.

Was there a way to resolve such troubling possibilities? *In Memory of the Life in Paradise (Souvenir de la vie du paradis)* (1946), a fantasy piece, Duhamel wrote of the experiences of Sebastien, who left the earth to fly to heaven. As he traveled through space, through the galaxies, Sebastien felt extreme relaxation and pleasure. "I feel so very well! I'm so happy! It isn't natural!"[9] When he arrived in heaven, however, things took on a different hue. He saw God and very soon afterward realized that He too was plagued with problems, that unhappiness was rampant, as well as joy. Sebastien met Job who adored his God and who felt uplifted in His presence; he met Noah who had been given an extra kingdom for the fine services he had rendered to God; he saw his mother who wept in sadness because her husband could not join her since he had been sent to another domain—hell—for his infidelities. What Sebastien found in heaven, however, did not satisfy him, and he realized that actually this realm, considered for so long to be ideal, was merely a replica of earth on a larger and more spacious scale, ruled with greater vigor.

The notion of utopia, which Duhamel had clung to for so many years, even during his Créteil days when he had founded the small colony of artists and literary men with his friend Charles Vildrac, was actually a figment of man's imagination. It would always remain in the realm of the abstract; it would never materialize. Yet, he maintained, one must not be deluded into considering everything on earth in a dismal manner. Even in the most horrendous of times, when persecutions and bloody wars were fomenting—during the Renaissance, for example—there were extraordinary figures such as Erasmus, real bringers of light.

In *Sowing in the Wind (Semailles au vent)* (1947), a series of essays, Duhamel describes Erasmus, among others, whose works have remained as vital and as important in his time as they did during the Renaissance period. Erasmus was a fighter for the mind—for free thought. The tool of reason permitted him to live life fully and to express his thoughts powerfully, in allegorical terms, frequently during periods when freedom of speech was sharply curtailed. Cervantes was another writer whom Duhamel deeply admired. Though this Spaniard spent many years in prison and was really not a heroic figure, Don Quixote was edifying, consoling, moralistic, and able to afford people great pleasure centuries after he had been created. Essays on Anatole France, Henri de Régnier, Paul Valéry, Jean Richard Bloch, and others whom Duhamel greatly admired also figured in *Sowing to the Wind.*

France was mending. Her people were working arduously to rebuild, to make up for the time lost, to heal the wounds. In *Herbarium and Bestiary (Le Bestiaire et l'herbier)* (1948), a charming work dedicated to Jean Rostand, Duhamel describes his feelings in terms of animals and flowers, all the shrubs within his entourage—the snail who is courageous and who is to be pitied at the same time; the fly who is noisy, brutal, and at times frenzied; dogs, squirrels, cats, children, mothers, fathers. Each of the vignettes has a moral: the tomato, for example, which grows and grows until it bursts—with pride. One of the most poignant statements, however, concerns a friend who had hurt Duhamel years and years before and had lacerated his heart.

When the friend whom I loved hurt me, betrayed me, when I had to renounce this attachment, a work which had begun in my youth, when I was forced to break the chains which had given me so much pleasure, I thought that nothing could assuage my pain, no foreseeable remedy could be found. . . .

Then the years passed, some galloping at a furious rate, others creeping along. The war tormented the world. . . . Empires have fallen amid clouds of dust.

The old wound has closed, the one I had thought incurable. Some days I even forget it, for days on end, something which I must admit, humiliated me. Then I look at my wound and I reproach it.[10]

CHAPTER 8

Despair—Hope

S EVERAL TYPES OF NOVELS have flourished in France since
World War II: psychological and antipsychological; those with plots
and the plotless; novels with faceless characters and those having
recognizable identities. It was as if the floodgates hampering the free
flow of literary creativity had suddenly been removed and works with
variegated esthetics gushed forth with unparalleled vigor. Sartre and
Camus novelized their wartime experiences, each describing within a
semirealistic framework his own existential view of mankind, his disgust
and hatred for the status quo. Boris Vian, Marguerite Duras, Jean
Genet, Samuel Beckett broke with the traditional novel structure, that
of the well-made plot, with its linear time concepts and conventional
character types. The "New Novelists" (a convenient title given a group
of disparate literary innovators which include such names as Nathalie
Sarraute, Alain Robbe-Grillet, Claude Simon, Michel Butor, Robert
Pinget) rejected traditional techniques—analytically or psychologically
constructed characters. They endeavored to discover a new reality,
more profound for them than the one depicted heretofore in literature.
Other authors, more conventional by nature, pursued the same courses
they had followed since they began writing: Georges Duhamel, Jean
Giono, Georges Bernanos.

During the 1950's Duhamel's novels *Patrice Périot (Le Voyage de
Patrice Périot)* (1950), *Cry out of the Depths (Cri des profondeurs)*
(1951), *The Voyagers of Hope (Les Voyageurs de l'Espérance)* (1953),
The Archangel of Adventure (L'Archange de l'aventure) (1956), *The
Companions of the Apocalypse (Les Compagnons de l'apocalypse)*
(1956), and *Théophile's Complex (Le Complexe de Théophile)* (1958)
were all written in the traditional manner. Each volume was armed with
a plot, and each included one or two main characters upon whom
attention was focused; these protagonists were psychologically constructed and were revealed as recognizable flesh-and-blood human

143

beings; time sequences were linear; the framework was realistic. Though nothing was altered structurally, the topics upon which Duhamel focused his attention did vary.

Duhamel's postwar novels centered almost exclusively upon matters of religion: God, the soul, evil, human destiny. These basic questions were probed, sounded out by Duhamel, with renewed dynamism. The urgency with which he questioned, however, resulted most certainly from the suffering he had witnessed about him during and after the second great holocaust. Though he had been exposed to atrocities in World War I Duhamel reacted to the horrors perpetrated upon humanity in the 1930s and 1940s as would a young man filled with hope for the future and the enthusiasm necessary to build a new world. In 1919 he had possessed the resiliency of youth. After World War II, however, Duhamel was over sixty years of age, and life had taken on a very different hue. Though he still maintained "hope"—that is, he believed in man's ability to establish a world fit to live in, at least temporarily—his prognosis for humanity's future as a whole was not optimistic. "HOPE EVEN SO! A despairing hope, he heard a voice say from the depths of his being."[1] Duhamel was, furthermore, certain that a confrontation between two opposing ideologies was going to occur and that, after the detonation and proliferation of atomic bombs, man's survival on earth might no longer be possible.

I Patrice Périot

Patrice Périot narrates the story of a biologist. A hard worker, an idealist, Périot is, at the same time, extraordinarily naive in political matters. He believes that by signing all types of manifestos, which he never even takes the trouble to read, the world will be a better place in which to live. As is to be expected, the various societies and movements which he has endorsed take advantage of his name to pursue their own left-wing causes. Patrice Périot's family situation fares no better. A widower, he devotes all of his time to his research work and little to his four children who live with him. He fails, therefore, to establish any kind of workable relationship with them. Edwige, thirty years old, is married to a prosaic and uninspiring creature; Christine is a Communist, Thierry a devout Catholic, Hervé a poet who commits suicide because he is too fearful to confess his gambling debts to his father. Disconsolate over his son's demise, Périot searches, with Thierry's help, for an answer in God—or in the eternal mystery which is the world.

The themes with which Duhamel is preoccupied in *Patrice Périot* are clearly similar in nature to those he treated in *The Masters* and in *The Stormy Night:* the man whose life revolves solely around science, who is unable to communicate with others, who has rejected the spiritual aspects of existence. Patrice, ostrichlike, buries his head in sand (his work), thereby clouding his vision to such an extent that he becomes unable to see the world crumbling about him. Had he applied some of his scientific acumen to the realm of daily existence, he might have fared better. He certainly would have read the manifestos he signed, discussed and probed various situations rather than remaining aloof. Because of his lack of insight into mundane matters, he destroys rather than constructs, hinders those very economic and political causes in which he believes and inadvertently brings about the death of his own son.

Duhamel believed that a scientist should devote the bulk of his energies to his research work, that his world should be free from political pressures, but that, by the same token, he should not cut himself off from life's mainstream. Patrice Périot is forever complaining of the many demands made upon him. He is overburdened, he says, with laboratory work, plagued by masses of mail he feels compelled to answer, invitations he always seeks to refuse, political manifestos which are constantly being brought to him. He is submerged in work, however, because he wants to be. Unconsciously speaking, work is a device to avoid the conflicts presented by daily life. Work becomes his refuge, his realm. The older he grows, the more compulsive is his attitude toward the laboratory. Indeed, he hardly ever lives or breathes away from it. He probably feels—if he ever thought of it at all—that his family will grow strong without his help as does an olive tree. What he fails to perceive is that a tree also needs care; otherwise it may become lopsided, even stunted.

There are reasons, excuses perhaps, which would explain Périot's frenetic attitude toward his work. He came from a poor family of small artisans. His parents worked long hours to save enough money to put him through school. He studied arduously and has worked ever since he was a young lad to supplement his tiny income. If he ever slackens in his work habits, he must fear, unconsciously, that he will be overcome with guilt feelings. As time passes, work becomes routine, habitual, and no more thought is given to changing his way of life.

Périot is imbued with fine qualities, despite his one-sided nature. He is a tender, sensitive, and deeply humanitarian being. He wants to see "happiness" dispensed about him. He cannot tolerate poverty or suffering. Because of such profound brotherly notions, he seeks to help all worthy groups. "Even if I risk making a mistake, I am going to sign, I will sign. It is better to make a mistake and do what is necessary so that one will never have to reproach oneself."[2] Only when he learns from the newspapers that his name has been used to further the cause of the extreme Left—which he never condoned—does he realize the vastness of his mistake. Then he suffers from acute feelings of *malaise*. His unwillingness to learn about the movements he has endorsed results in his despair, in negative rather than positive results.

Périot's family situation is even more dismal. Christine, the Communist, rejects all conventions—even the father image, such as it is. She is hard to approach and has built a carapace around her. She can no longer react to family or to friends. She lives in her own limited realm, repudiating the bourgeois family situation. Though she knows she will be hurting her father deeply, she informs him suddenly and brazenly that she will never marry, that she is taking a lover instead. Frequently, she even looks upon her father with expressions of hatred. Indeed, she so despises everything he stands for that she even refuses to be called by her Christian name, chosing another, Vera, instead.

The most heartrending of the children is Hervé, the poet. Weakly structured, he lives in an isolated realm, unable to communicate his sorrow to a living being. Devoid of any motivating force in the world, he is, nevertheless, imbued with a profound sense of right and wrong. Because he feels such guilt at being unable to pay his gambling debts, because he is unable to confide in his father or anyone else, he can do nothing but further the destructiveness in which he had been indulging since he was a child. Life for him is filled with strangers; he can no longer bear the agony of his despair and solitude.

Perhaps the most interesting character, from a philosophical point of view, is Thierry. His religiousness is as extreme as his father's work in the laboratory. Both are escape mechanisms. Thierry, in effect, rejects life for an eternal world of the spirit. His great joy occurs, he says, when he prays. His face then takes on a certain triumph, a radiance which is truly otherwordly. His face, Périot declares, is "filled with esctasy, sunshine, cut only with a smile radiating happiness."[3] The father watches his son during those moments he is communing with God. He reasons, however, that although religion has brought ineffable joy to his son, such an attitude cannot be an answer to his problems. An overly cerebral or scientific attitude is as limiting and eventually as destructive as a totally religious one. A conciliation, therefore, has to be effected between the two extremes so that a positive point of view—balance and harmony—can come to pass. "One must reconcile intelligence with life, reason with joy." Patrice cannot and will not act hypocritically toward his son. He expresses his feeling on this subject openly and succinctly. He cannot embrace a religion in which he does not believe. He will therefore go *his* way alone, suffer his anguish and affliction, the infinite remorse he feels after Hervé's suicide. After he has spoken to his son in this fashion, Périot feels unburdened and strengthened, even by adversity. He will pursue his life's cause "until the hour of destiny, persevere in love and even in hope."[4]

If we look upon the character Patrice Périot as a mirror image of Duhamel, we become aware of the pressing questions he was asking himself at this period. He was searching for answers to his own spiritual needs, to humanity's distress. He tried to comprehend the vast mysteries of human existence, man in his most sordid and in his most beautiful aspects. Duhamel, an agnostic his whole life, did not and could not become a member of a church. He was not religious in the conventional Catholic manner. He did believe in an Eternal Force and with fervor. He felt compelled to probe his beliefs, to sound out his own depths, to find the God within. What better way for Duhamel to perform such a feat than to create living beings in the process of such discovery?

From a literary point of view, *Patrice Périot* might be considered a bit banal, since it treats a worn theme: the father who fails to bring up his children properly, who devotes an inordinate amount of time to his work. The suicide of Périot's son may be considered a trifle melodramatic to sophisticated readers these days. The characters, nevertheless, are sharply delineated and their points of view incised with warmth.

II Cry out of the Depths

A preoccupation with God also obsesses Duhamel in *Cry out of the Depths*. The novel takes place during the German occupation of France. Félix Tallemand, the central figure, is a collaborator who seeks to give the impression of being honorable and righteous, of being on the side of justice and of God. As the novel begins, Félix is only an employee in the firm of Dardelle, Winterberg Company. He seeks to gain control of it. When war breaks out and France loses, he wants people to think he is helping his boss, Winterberg, his family. He knows, however, through his collaborator friend, Abel Zamian, that the Winterbergs will be caught by the Nazis and sent to a concentration camp. Events occur in just this fashion. Only the father Winterberg survives; his wife and children are exterminated. He returns to Paris only a few days before the liberation. Since Félix risks nothing, he hides Winterberg in his cellar, giving the impression of great heroism. Félix has committed other wrongs: toward his brother; toward his wife, for whom he felt no real affection; and toward his daughter, by not permitting her to marry the man she loves. When Félix is about to die, he feels something stir within him—anguish—his *conscience.*

Cry out of the Depths is a profound study of a coward type. Félix is a man who refuses to admit his weakness, prefers deceit to the difficulties involved when facing life truthfully. Félix' first wish is to *appear* righteous. Whatever he does—providing it takes place beneath this façade—is immaterial to him. Appearances are his sole preoccupation. The core of man, Félix' inner world, must of necessity remain hidden. "My main idea is to act according to the regulations, to be irreproachable. That's it. I am irreproachable. It's not a type of superstition, but rather my own personal religion."[5] Félix' behavior is unwavering. He never stops to consult his heart or his conscience. He is by nature a pragmatist whose goal—to become director of a business— justifies the means.

Politically speaking, Félix dislikes anything that disturbs the status quo, anything that might hamper his own field of action, his economic aggrandizement. He is always on the winning side. When, for example, he becomes aware of the fact that war is in store for France, he suddenly voices his dissatisfaction with French politicians, castigating their timid stand before the enemy, during the crucial years preceding the conflagration. They have followed, he maintains, a defensive policy rather than attempting a vigorous and aggressive one which would have enabled France to attack outright. Such statements are all show. Félix has no intention of doing anything for his country, either before the hostilities begin or after. During those all-too-important years before World War II, Félix went along with all French policy; he never advocated belligerence, but rather a timid and "peaceful" program. Now he knows clearly that he runs no risks. By condemning his previous attitude, he finds himself once again reiterating what the majority thinks. France, Félix reasons, will be on her knees in a matter of days; the Jews will be persecuted immediately and forced to give up their businesses and their lives; and he, Félix, will be able to take over the entire firm with great ease.

After France has been defeated, Félix' brother—a patriot—asks him what his attitude is to be: to go along with the German occupying force or to work against it? Félix responds in a matter of seconds. Using the most casuistic type of reasoning, in order to prevent his brother from suspecting his real motivations, he lets it be known that he will do nothing contrary to the demands made upon him by the government. Félix then proceeds to become master of the business firm. He succeeds and walks with head held high. He needs the admiration of others in order to fully enjoy the money and power which have now accrued to him. Such a necessity is made manifest when he says to himself: "I was tempted to inform him that I was no longer the unimportant brother, the employee, the poor relative."[6]

Never once does Félix question the validity or the moral integrity of his actions. He is aware of the fact that he is the harbinger of death, evil, and doom—that greed has prodded him on. These character traits and responsibilities stir nothing within him. Winterberg and his family are sent to Drancy and put to death, and all this is attributable, indirectly, to Félix. Because Winterberg is only half Jewish, he is permitted to return to Paris. Félix then displays "great" kindness, first by hiding him, then by giving him ten shares of the company's stock. In this way, Winterberg will not starve and Félix will be the recipient of his gratitude. After this show of "generosity," however, Félix' inner voice speaks forth: "This way we're quits! I'll have some peace in this way. I'm acting according to the rules!"[7] Despite this grandiose act, Félix is in some small way showing some signs of crumbling, of experiencing anguish—even a particle of guilt. Something within him is finally stirring. His conscience is no longer dormant but is heaving a bitter—if an inaudible—sigh. It is going to be difficult to deal with such a force. Félix, who has now amassed some wealth, can *enjoy* neither his material possessions nor his social gains:

No one can help me. The nightmare is becoming painful. What is this thing which lives within us, which thinks and which suffers without asking us for our advice, without taking into consideration the least warning, of our ways, our ruses, our decisions? Almost every night now I awaken with a start, and I begin to speak out when I'm alone.[8]

Only when Félix is about to die does the full weight of his conscience come to the fore. The shock of his sordid actions, of his ruthlessness and cruelty toward all those who love him, creates havoc within his being. The greater Félix' agony and turmoil and the kinder are those caring for him, the greater is his own trial and pain.

"Everyone has forgiven me. But there is someone, or something, in my depths, which does not forgive."[9] Who is this mysterious someone who refuses to pardon Félix? His conscience, most certainly, is unwilling to grant him peace before death. It rejects the superficial and contrived excuses Félix has always found to explain his deeds—deeds which could never be undone. At the end, his agony is so great he finally is compelled to face the lesions within his own character, to admit that he has put the Winterbergs to death, that he has destroyed his daughter's life and his wife's also.

Duhamel's keen description of Félix' growing guilt feelings is quite extraordinary. Like Salavin who seeks saintliness, so Félix seeks power and adulation. Neither character achieves his goal. Both men are fearful of facing themselves, of revealing their inner nature, their weaknesses. Both seek excuses, explanations for their ways. Though Salavin is fully aware of the dichotomy within his personality—and from the very beginning—his means of altering his condition is inadequate because his reasoning is faulty. Salavin is a man incapable of action, powerless to the extreme. Félix is, in this respect, his counterpart. He is energetic, capable, but dispenses with all morality. Moreover, he never admits to the division within his own being, to his pragmatic tendencies. Both men, however, are in the last analysis molded of the same stuff: introverted, self-centered, egotistical, repudiating all the love and affection showered upon them. What differentiates them most strongly is the fact that Félix is obsessed with *appearances,* whereas Salavin has no interest in façades at all.

What is arresting in *Cry out of the Depths,* aside from its analytical descriptions, is Duhamel's depiction of the plight of the Jews during the war. The sensitivity and understanding he displays when portraying Winterberg's growing despair, his total dedication to his family, is unparalleled. In the beginning of the novel, we are introduced to a hard-working Winterberg, a good father, a fine human being in his social and business relations. As the war progresses, he becomes increasingly more haggard and secretive. Finally, in a show of anguish, he confesses his financial plight to Félix and informs him of his desire to flee Paris, to reach the unoccupied zone. There is a tradition, Winterberg confesses, among Jews: they must always be prepared to leave a land—even at a moment's notice—and for this reason they must be able to carry their worldly possessions on their backs. The fruit of spiritual labor, therefore, must always reside within the individual, his values, if intellectual and moral, and his talents must be able to be put to use in any kind of society; his dynamism must be made to succeed in whatever endeavor he chooses. The material wealth of the Jew, Winterberg declares, must of necessity consist of jewels which can be hidden and transported with ease.[10] Though Winterberg loved books, music, and paintings, he thought it wise to convert these objects into pearls and diamonds so that he can leave with his family for safer quarters. The pathetic love he displays vis-à-vis his family is described with tenderness; Duhamel is never maudlin, never indulges in bathos. When his family is taken to Drancy he refuses to leave them; he offers his life for theirs. After the war, when the story is told by others, even the collaborator, Zamian, confesses that Winterberg acted with courage, like a true Corneillian hero, implying by this statement the vast differences existing between Félix and Winterberg.

Duhamel's acute understanding of problems facing minorities, particularly those undergoing persecution, his ability to portray their anguishes and torments, is one aspect of the extreme compassion he feels for all humanity.

III   The Voyagers of Hope

The Voyagers of Hope could be looked upon as a modern rendition of the Noah myth. After an atomic blast, very nearly the entire world is covered with water. The Fromond family finds safety in their ship, *Hope*. They travel about for some time and finally reach a mountain peak (which could be looked upon as a twentieth-century Mount Ararat), where they decide to make their new home. They begin life anew, as had Noah and his sons had done. They fish, plant a garden, and become relatively self-sufficient. They do not live an isolated existence, however, but observe the world about them in order to learn whatever they can. In one adventure, they notice an entire area filled with dead fish, monsters, and a type of land formation which in no way resembles what they used to know. On another occasion, they see an entire city—churches, homes, public areas, streets and so on—covered with water. They realize that if they are to survive they must begin to work the land they have chosen to inhabit, take advantage of the fish surrounding it, and try to gather from nature what is beneficial to them. Their dictum is: "To work! Our life is in front of us. We have many obligations."

Though primarily a work of fantasy, designed to entertain children, Duhamel nevertheless confronts highly pressing problems, those facing us today in the atomic age. If bombs are detonated, Duhamel maintains, man will have to pay the consequences. Though havoc will be wreaked upon humanity, these same forces of destruction can be mastered and put to good use. A new generation may find a way of founding a fresh existence based on truth, friendship, and good will. In ancient times, man was punished for having transgressed the word of God, for having immersed himself in evil—Noah alone was saved. Today, the situation has altered: man will destroy himself. It is he, not God, who is responsible for his doom. Because man believes he can order the cosmos to suit his purposes, because of his extreme inflation and the pride he has taken in his scientific achievements, he has paved the way for an imbalance in the world and in his own psyche. Man's moral, esthetic, spiritual, and intellectual forces are at odds with each other. Chaos is the only alternative, after which, hopefully, balance will return.

Duhamel's outlook, though rather bleak for the immediate future, is, as it had been during biblical times, better for the long run. The question remaining in Duhamel's mind is the following: will man know how to make the most of the opportunity offered him—or will he commit the same mistakes ad infinitum?

IV   The Archangel of Adventure

The Archangel of Adventure is once again centered upon the subject of faith. Cyprien Ricord, a happily married painter, meets Mikael, who takes him to the United States to enjoy the commercial fruits of his labor. Once success is his, Mikael runs away with Cyprien's wife. Alone, the painter discovers his faith through his son, for whom he only now realizes the depth of his love. For the first time Cyprien enjoys true happiness.

The Archangel of Adventure touches upon Duhamel's bête noire: the machine age. His distaste for its hideousness is now carried into the artist's domain. The constant publicity, the loud speakers, the mass media which bombard Cyprien Ricord once he arrives in the United States make it impossible for him to experience even the slightest peace of mind. Nor can he indulge in fruitful meditation. Moreover, the speed, the superficiality of the flashy existence he leads in this land indicate the emptiness of those who cultivate such an atmosphere.

Mikael's presence in the novel is of utmost importance. He is the catalyzing agent, the force which propels Cyprien Ricord into this turbulent and abysmal realm. Cyprien would have continued to live out his relatively happy existence as a mediocre painter, with his wife and son. Mikael, the Archangel–God's messenger, symbolically speaking–arrives on the scene and forces Cyprien to *act*. Though Mikael's attitude might seem to be cruel at first, Cyprien might never have found *himself*, that inner being he had neglected for so long or had perhaps never even encountered, had Mikael not compelled him to suffer.

Mikael describes himself in the following manner: "Every day I kill a monster and every day I celebrate the joy of life, of dreaming, of surpassing oneself, of being very nearly a God."[11] The monster Mikael kills is the man Cyprien was when he lived in ignorant bliss. Before he knew pain, passion, or joy, Cyprien had experienced only a peripheral existence, never a real one. Cyprien has never been forced to choose in life, to probe, not even in the domain of art. He is what Sartre calls a *"salaud,"* a man who has never experienced the anguish of "nausea," the trauma every sensitive individual knows when forced to face the reality of an absurd existence.

Even Cyprien's marriage is based on an unsteady foundation. It is bathed in happy mediocrity. His wife cannot understand her husband's artistic temperament, and he never bothers to ponder her personality. She lives on the surface of things. She helps him, to be sure, but only in a most shallow manner. Neither husband nor wife ever taps the depths of being, ever confronts each other or any issue or touches that meaningful nerve which cements relationships, which dredges up that material which can later be molded by the artist into a masterpiece. Once Cyprien Ricord's wife has been removed from his world, the pain he encounters does away with the protective buffer zone which she represents. He has to face the world himself. New feelings, fresh ways of perceiving existence, come into consciousness. The inner turbulence spurs on his painting. He discovers new color tones, new depths which help him create the masterpiece he paints at the end of the book.

There is no question about Cyprien Ricord's talent. He knows how to paint. He is well aware of this fact. He believes sincerely that a painter should be able to force a spectator to reconstruct within himself an entire world after viewing a tableau. Until Cyprien has come into contact with true reality–that God within–he merely paints works which appeal to snobs: pleasant, attractive, relatively meaningless visual designs. His work is popular and sells well. Never, however, has he stirred those smoldering depths. Only at the end, when painting his son playing in the sand, does he bring forth that *Deus absconditus* from within and place it in an understandable form on canvas. He succeeds in creating the true work of art because he has reached within, linking up inner and outer man. He has discovered his *religion,* which is defined as "a linking back." Now, serenity will be his. In addition to this feeling of well-being, there is the discovery of a new domain, capable of enriching his existence. To communicate with those eternal elements within mankind—to be able to transform this amorphous entity onto canvas—is to succeed in grasping the true meaning of life through art. It is thus through pain and by means of his love for his son that he discovers himself, humanity, and those universal forces.

Duhamel's positive ending in *The Archangel of Adventure* is another indication of his own positive understanding of pain. He felt that anguish, when looked upon as a fecundating force, can unleash profound meanings which might never have been discovered without chaos. It is not by adhering to the limiting forces of organized religion that Cyprien Ricord discovers eternity in the work of art but rather through contact with nature in its most basic form—the child. It is through the child that he comes to know purity of soul and touches God. The intellect, of which the adult is usually the slave or which he most frequently considers to be the *sine qua non* of life, is a deterrent in many cases to the discovery of true existence. In order to live fully, one must coexist with the *feeling* principle in man. The child in *The Archangel of Adventure* comes to represent purity as well as the feeling principle. Once contact is made with him, the unity within Cyprien Ricord's personality can be achieved.

Duhamel relates the discovery of Cyprien Ricord's innermost self in a simple and straightforward manner, without having recourse to an overly complicated plot line. Even the characters are not overly dense and evolve in a realistic manner.

V   The Companions of the Apocalypse

The Companions of the Apocalypse, by comparison with the preceding novels, seems artificial and contrived. The exaggeration in character analyses, the religious notions discussed, are very nearly ludicrous.

The Companions of the Apocalypse concerns a war veteran who seeks to convert the world to his Christian ethics. He calls himself Dan Traveler and preaches his credo together with his disciples who worship him as a virtual deity. Dan foresees the end of the world as prophesied in the Book of Revelation. In all of his impassioned speeches, which are certainly modeled after certain American evangelists, he begs man to change his sinful ways and to adhere to the ways of the Lord. At first he is greeted with applause and admiration in the small towns he visits. As time goes on, however, the nature of his reception alters. Indeed, the townspeople begin to mock him and his disciples. At the end of the novel, one of the disciples dies and two others leave him to continue living normal lives. Finally, Dan decides to give up his mission in life. He leaves his worldly goods to his remaining followers.

Dan Traveler is a man imbued with the conviction that he is a prophet—perhaps even a reincarnation of Christ. His entire demeanor resembles his conception of Christ. Moreover, his disciples adore him in much the same fashion as Christ's did. They share in all worldly goods; they practice acts of kindliness as they understand them. They are even jealous at times of their master's affection for one or the other; each frequently vies for the master's love. Dan's mission, as he conceives of it, is certainly not to entertain or to amuse the various townspeople who listen to him preach but rather to instruct them, to enlighten them. He is a believer in the letter of the Bible and is convinced beyond doubt that man's presence on this planet is doomed to oblivion. He warns his listeners of this eventuality and asks them all to beg God's forgiveness before it is too late. Ambition, he declares, must be annihilated in each being; passion must be reasoned and power curtailed.

The most—perhaps only—interesting part of this novel lies in Dan's conversations about religion, first with a priest he meets and then with a doctor. Dan condemns the man whose belief is limited to church law, whose sight is very nearly nil, whose imagination is constrained. The priest is such a man. He refuses to help any religious group or any religion which might further schisms within the church. He decries individual thought or personal belief in a dogma not in conformity with Roman Catholicism. Only in union is man's salvation possible, he claims. As for the doctor, his mode of thinking is equally distasteful to Dan. The scientist's rational view is nefarious and constricting, since he does not take into account man's spiritual or emotional tendencies.

For Dan, prayer is man's way to salvation. Saint John, he declares, had a vision of the world once it is abandoned to madmen and to extremists and felt himself destined to prepare humanity for what lay in store. Man must change, Dan declares. He must view existence in a more profound and meaningful way. Peace, respect of beings, goodness must be restored to this world.[12] Dan is the man to enforce these notions.

Dan's message in the final analysis goes unheeded. Such an outcome is not unusual, however, since all innovators suffer the rebuff of the masses. Those who *see* have always been rejected. Cassandra, for example, warned the Trojans to beware of the Greek horse. Her prognostications went unheeded. The vast difference between Dan and the missionaries and prophets of old is that Dan becomes discouraged and does not fight to see his ideal through until death. As long as his message is greeted with admiration, as it was in the beginning, he feels strong, certain of his attitudes. Slowly, however, as audiences become less and less enthusiastic about him and his view of humanity and the world at large, Dan becomes intimidated, fearful, unsure of his approach. After his disciples' departure, he further questions his acts and values. He searches desperately for an answer and begs God for a response. He prays. He bemoans the fact that he has suffered the anguish destined for the leader, that he is misunderstood and mocked. He also suffers personal pain with the death of his "beloved disciple." When, at the end of the novel, Dan accepts the fact that his mission has been a failure, his suffering intensifies. He succumbs to sleep finally, but in this realm a voice keeps repeating: "Tell me that I am not mistaken! Give me your approbation!"[13] He begs God, with all the power within him—within his body and soul—to communicate with him. When he awakens from his sleep, steps outside of the house, stands in front of the church, he murmurs his prayer once again. He begs God to let him know whether he has endured enough to obtain His pardon and His attention.[14] At that very instant Dan hears a sigh, the autumn wind rushing around the stone edifice—God's domain—and he hears His answer clearly: "Yes . . . yes . . . yes. . . ." Relieved by this show of mercy, this expression of supreme understanding, Dan turns toward the wind and murmurs his "thank you," his gratitude, and then walks away "at the mercy of the night, the last breath on his lips, the supreme prayer emanating from his dolorous soul, finally delivered from life and dreams."[15]

Duhamel's concept of God, as we have already seen expressed in his other novels, is not limited to a specific credo; neither the doctor nor the priest can quench Duhamel's feelings for the Eternal Force. Duhamel's God is all-embracing, completely free from the shackles which man imposes upon Him as he sets out to codify and dogmatize what is essentially a cosmic phenomenon—unlimited, omnipotent, and omniscient. Duhamel's God communicates with all men and without the help of ministers or priests. He is devoid of the hatreds implicit in man's religious credos, rules, regulations, and other binding forces. Duhamel's religion is personal and poignant—eternally present. It is based on fraternity, on goodness and understanding of the needs and desires of others. Unlike organized religion which has so blatantly preached hatred rather than love, the sword rather than the plowshare, anger rather than serenity, Duhamel's view is motivated by his spiritual probings as well as by his balanced and harmonious personality. He bears no grudges, psychologically speaking, and so cannot project hatred onto any religious concept.

Dan, in many ways is Duhamel, traveling about the world, confronting opposing forces and facing up to God alone at the end, able to discern his inner voice through the wind, considered symbolically to represent the Spirit or God's breath.

Other aspects of *The Companions of the Apocalypse* do not measure up to the portrait Duhamel draws of Dan. In terms of character, his disciples offer no interest whatsoever. First, they seem to be placed in a variety of artificial situations. Second, they are depicted as a group of lost children traveling in the wilderness; they are like bleating lambs without any sense at all; they have no identity and are incapable of doing anything except loving their master and vying for his affection. In many ways they seem to be throwbacks to some primitive itinerant group, some medieval vestige, similar in many respects to the helpers of mountebanks. These groups would come into town and preach first, then try to sell their miraculous product—the elixir of youth—the one answer to all problems. The attitude, the language, the gestures of Dan's disciples verge on the humorous. They are not only infantile in their demeanor and their thought processes; they seem veritably devoid of any intelligence whatsoever—retarded, indeed.

The Companions of the Apocalypse may be viewed as a satire on modern evangelical movements, aimed also at self-styled missionaries who parade about the land preaching their "wares," whatever these may be, imposing their thoughts, fears, and dicta on the naive, the innocent, or even the highly bigoted. Only Dan's inner evolution can be taken seriously in this work.

VI Théophile's Complex

Théophile's Complex is not only an interesting volume but a sophisticated one as well. Again we confront a Salavin-type creature. Théophile suffers from egoism, introversion, and extreme vanity. What turns his life into a horrendous experience is his awareness of the evils lodged within his character. These are forever rising up to plague him. Théophile would like to be like other men but is unable to model himself upon them. He is, therefore, incapable of altering his acts, his course, or his thinking process. His world revolves in an endless and vicious circle.

Théophile lives with his sister, whom he adores. He is employed by an airline company, and his only friend is a pilot who suffers from perpetual bouts of depression. Théophile believes in God. The pilot is convinced that God is something personal and possessive, that He belongs to him alone, that He watches over his every act and thought. When the pilot suspects that God has abandoned him, he wants to die. He accepts a job which will end in his death. He hires himself out as a pilot to a group who seeks to kill a certain politician. The irony of the story resides in the fact that all aboard the plane die save the politician. Théophile is the one who has negotiated the entire deal, and he is tortured thereafter with feelings of guilt.

The plot of *Théophile's Complex* is slight. The interest in this work revolves around the protagonist's analysis of himself and his concept of God. Théophile's confessor is convinced that he is an unbeliever because the idea of "nothingness" is intolerable to him. Théophile declares that he prefers hell to the void.[16] Because he has led a sheltered existence, he is unable to cope with life. At forty-five he still lives calmly, docilely under his sister's protective wing. He considers her a saint and has never made a decision without first consulting her. He has, therefore, never engaged himself in the mainstream of life. He is, psychologically, a dwarfed or stunted being.

His negotiation of the deal in which his pilot friend is to die is the only act he ever commits on his own. Before going through with the negotiations, he discusses his friend's emotional stand and spiritual notions. These are complex and difficult for Théophile to accept and assimilate. His friend, Himer, however, has utter confidence in a *personal* God, that is, one whose function is to preoccupy himself entirely and exclusively with him. Himer does not believe in a religion in which all people are involved. Though religion means "that which binds or links back," and though he does go to church to pray, Himer's God does not belong to others. He loves Jesus, Himer declares, in his own way, but *his* Jesus and not Théophile's.[17] When Himer gambles, as he does frequently, since this is his favorite pastime, he is at the mercy of a passion and calls upon his God for assistance. Then he does not pray in this fashion; he assumes the expression of a saint, "when he cast his golden louis into the air which helped him solve—several of life's problems."[18] Here Duhamel is most definitely satirizing the concept of sainthood and the saint, with his holy attitudes, his utter self-centeredness, his possessiveness concerning God.

Théophile implored God to help him understand his friend, to illuminate him, to succeed in reasoning with the "unreasonable Himer."[19] As introverted and egotistical in his own way as Himer is in his, Théophile is convinced that God has placed his friend in his path so as to test his faith.[20] Though Théophile does not consider himself a saint, had God infused this holy feeling within him, he declares, he would have been eternally grateful. "Notice that when saying this, I am not accusing the Almighty of being capricious or arbitrary. He knows us better than we know ourselves."[21]

Strangely enough, after Théophile realizes that he has been the accomplice to a murder, that he has actually been the go-between for the two factions, he does not suffer the agony of guilt. He felt destined, he reasons, to perform this deed, because he was truly helping his friend Himer who had—finally—believed that God had abandoned him. Once Himer became aware of his own solitude, of God's rejection of him, he could not face life. Théophile, therefore, was in reality performing a kind deed, helping his friend reach that realm of eternal bliss—death. To have concluded thusly, however, means that Théophile has finally wrestled with his feelings, that he feels, "miraculously" enough, invaded by a calm, a a "strange nocturnal slumber."[22] He realizes that whatever he has tried to understand about him, about life and humanity in general, is of little import. He can rise above the petty details of life, become detached from everyone, except from his own being—and of course his sister Béatrice whom he adores. Once Théophile has been invaded—or thinks he has—by God's presence, he concludes that faith does not merely consist in reciting a series of prayers or litanies learned in childhood, but rather means a type of aspiration or elevation "toward a being whom we must not try to describe or paint, toward a world where the best in us will find its refuge and its reason for existing."[23] Hope alone remains for Théophile, that feeling injected into man by the Eternal Abstract Force—God.

Though *Théophile's Complex* was constructed as a novel, with characters and a well-knit plot, its purpose certainly, in the main at least, was to debate philosophical questions. For Théophile, God is both personal and impersonal, neither limited to one set of dogmas or another: He is an entity whose fire and brilliance permeates every aspect of the cosmos.

Duhamel's novels written during the 1950's center mostly around the Divine Principle: how it manifests itself in life, how various people conceive of this force, the theme of Evil. Certainly these preoccupations were experienced as part of the emotional aftermath of World War II.

The two most interesting novels of the group, *Patrice Périot* and *Cry out of the Depths,* deal with man's role within society, his career and family life, the differences which exist between outer and inner man—appearance and reality. These questions—existential in the main—had always preoccupied Duhamel, but seemed to be more urgently stated at this period. Duhamel was battling out these questions now, rethinking his role and function in society, trying to relate to his inner being, to the God within.

Certainly Duhamel must have felt himself to be—at least to a small extent—a missionary type. He took up the cause of man against the machine, of an abstract and all-encompassing God against the limited conceptions presented to man by organized religions, nature against the city. Each human being, however, must sound out his own soul, hear his own mind, dredge up from his own depths a philosophy in keeping with his personality—and with his life and times.

CHAPTER 9

Occidental Civilization Losing Ground

IN THE YEARS FOLLOWING World War II and throughout the 1950's, France experienced extreme fermentation and turmoil, both politically and economically. Duhamel, a man devoted to his country and people, could not help but feel the repercussions of such agitation. He was deeply concerned about the future. Rival ideologies vied with each other to gain supremacy over the minds of the apathetic—over the masses too.

At the very hour when I'm writing these pages . . . at this dramatic hour, the ship of the old Occidental Civilization is in a state of perdition. There is water everywhere. It has no more rudder nor lights. It wanders at the mercy of torments, horror and darkness.[1]

The Fourth Republic, which had been created shortly after the cessation of World War II, in 1946, suffered from instability. Indeed, it had no majority and met with serious, almost crucial problems during its twelve years of existence.

Perhaps France's most pressing question at this juncture was her colonial policy. Many French people were totally unaware of the spirit of revolt which had infiltrated both the African nations owned or protected by France and French Indochina. Many Frenchmen reasoned, and rightly so, that the Moroccans, Algerians, Senegalese, as well as other national and ethnic groups, had fought courageously on the side of the Allies during the second great holocaust. They, therefore, it was surmised, looked toward the mother country with devotion and pride. These same Frenchmen were totally unaware of the feelings of nationalism which were burgeoning in these newly "awakened" nations.

Bitter times were ahead. France's glorious years of colonial expansion were going to come to an abrupt and unpleasant end. Ever since 1881, when France had sent an expeditionary force to Tonkin and formed French Indochina, she had made her power known in that area. The tragedy of Dien Bien Phu in 1954 terminated France's possession there. Her occupation of North Africa, which had begun in 1830 with the first expeditionary corps sent to Algeria, had been an extremely fruitful one for both sides. Ties had been so closely knit for so many years that Algeria, like the motherland, was divided into departments. After World War II, however, various conflicting parties agitated. The colonists who were French by nationality and other immigrant groups, such as the Alsatians and Germans, did not want to loosen bonds with France. Indeed, each time mention was made of slackening such rapport, they felt abandoned and fearful. There were others, however, who sought to cut ties with the French: the FLN (Front de Libération Nationale) fought for total independence. The situation had reached such an impasse by 1958 that General de Gaulle, who had retired to his estate at Colombey-les-Deux-Eglises ever since his disagreement with the Assembly in 1946, was asked to head a new government. He would accept the offer, he declared, if certain conditions were met. The most important of these was constitutional reform. Such changes as he required were made and thus was born the Fifth Republic in 1958.

Though de Gaulle tried his best to remedy a highly charged state of affairs, he could do little to settle the strife. By 1961 the colonial situation had become so grave, the fighting so intense, that despite the government's advice, de Gaulle asked for a referendum to be taken in the various North African countries protected by France. The voters opted for independence. As a result, French North Africa severed all political ties with France, though economic and cultural relations remained strong.

I *Duhamel Travels*

Duhamel did not want to see France divested of her possessions. As a patriot, as one who had looked upon his country as a mighty power, he could not believe that the colonies wanted their freedom, nor did he believe they should be granted independence. He suggested, however, certain reforms: economic, cultural, and political. Moreover, he felt that the North African protectorates should become part of the French union and work together with the mother country in all domains.

Duhamel, as we have already noted, was no armchair philosopher. When he sensed trouble brewing, he decided to examine the situation for himself. In 1947, therefore, in order to gain firsthand information concerning North Africa, he and his wife set out on a trip which took them to Egypt, Lebanon, Tunisia, Algeria, Senegal, and Morocco. He not only interviewed people of note but talked with the colonists and with the simple folk. Thus, he mingled with both factions, those who voiced their unabashed admiration for the motherland; and with the others, whose hatred for France was so intense as to verge on the fanatical.

Duhamel's visit permitted him to study both sides of the question. He learned of the enormous contributions the French had made in these lands in terms of sanitation, agronomy, and education. He looked with pride to the fact that Arabs, trained in the French methods and graduates of French schools, produced far more and far greater amounts in their industrial and agricultural endeavors than those who had followed the ways of their ancestors. Duhamel, as was to be expected, was particularly interested in the medical reforms which France had introduced into these disease-ridden areas. As a result of French medical methods, the death rate had lessened considerably; the hospitals were better equipped, and cleanliness had been introduced. If France's influence were withdrawn, Duhamel reasoned, great suffering in all areas would ensue for the population of these lands.

Consultation on the Islamic Countries (Consultation aux pays d'Islam) (1947), written following his visit, is informative and interesting because of the precise economic, political, and cultural picture he draws for his readers. It was Duhamel's habit to try to include succinct historical and economic analysis of the lands he visited. This latest work was no exception. Duhamel first noted the rapid occidentalization which had taken place in the North African lands he visited and wondered whether the primitive multitudes, introduced as they had been to the latest mechanical inventions, would really benefit from this new way. Egypt was a case in point. It was growing at such a frenetic rate, Duhamel noted, that a tremendous imbalance made itself felt between technocracy and mechanization "for an elite" on the one side, and on the other extreme poverty and tribal ways for the masses. Were the natives ready for such mechanization, for such technical advances used frequently to perfection in highly developed lands? He wondered what the outcome would mean in terms of the well-being of the people involved. He was not sanguine.

When Duhamel and his wife returned to France, they knew in their hearts that their country was going to experience more bloodshed. They were more convinced than ever, however, that the North African protectorates should remain within the French fold, that these lands could and should benefit still further, as they had in the past, from such influence. The French language, after all, was spoken throughout North Africa; French culture permeated the society. Perhaps such an attitude was an overly romantic assessment of the situation. In many ways Duhamel had been blinded to the suffering, poverty, and dreadful diseases still rampant in these lands and which the French had not yet corrected. Like all colonists, the strong are guided principally by feelings of egotism: their goals are for the most part material; their control of the natives, ruthless. The French, in many cases, followed along these lines. They gained from the sweat of others, taking from the ignorant and weak, as did the powerful Arabs from their own people.

Man, whatever land he occupies, is motivated by selfish and material desires; his practices are for the most part ruthless. It is a question of human nature—no more, no less.

Duhamel did not limit his travels to North Africa. He went to the Orient as well. He had a veritable passion for traveling. He wanted to observe, to learn other ways of life. He also enjoyed the esthetic values inherent in traveling: experiencing the beauties of new landscapes and broadening, thereby, his own point of view. When in contact with other nations and different civilizations, Duhamel always tried to take in as much as he could, to assess the growth of various peoples, to compare their mores with his own.

In *Japan* (1953), Duhamel included sixty very interesting photographs which served to enhance an already fascinating volume. Duhamel began his travelogue in the usual fashion, with a historical picture of Japan, including a description of the Russo-Japanese War (1905), which dispelled any romantic notion concerning the Orient which Pierre Loti had introduced into his novels and which were, as a result, nurtured all those years.

Duhamel spent five weeks in Japan and visited as many cities as possible during his stay. He was amazed by the rapid growth of Japanese universities which, despite their increase, had become far too small for the overpopulated cities. Duhamel was veritably enraptured by the beauty of the landscape, its trees cut to all sizes and shapes, its rice paddies. The exquisite gardens with floral arrangements such as he had never seen before, by the people and their works: the colorful costumes worn by the natives and the art work created by both painters and sculptors. Duhamel, a gourmet, was also impressed by the delicious foods he tasted, the cooking habits of the families he visited, the place the mystical Zen ceremonies occupied in the serving of tea and in floral arrangements. He also visited theaters and saw the Kabuki and No players, the geisha girls entertaining in the various clubs. As was to be expected, Duhamel, a music lover, went to concerts and listened very carefully to the atonal Oriental music, so foreign to his Occidental ways. The temples and religious shrines where the devout prayed and meditated also lent enchantment to his stay. He noted with interest the extreme control and the physical prowess expended by the judo performances he saw.

There were moments when Duhamel was severely shocked. It was difficult for him to reconcile the tradition of good taste with the ugliness of the industrial society which had arisen with such furious gusto. The factories—he visited a paper factory—were unparalleled in ugliness, as were the many cities. Technology was responsible for such a state of affairs. This assessment of civilization was not new for Duhamel; he had been fighting industry's encroachment since the 1920's.

Japan, on the whole, is a rather superficial book. One cannot possibly appraise a country's work after only a five-week stay. Duhamel's works concerning North African countries, Germany, Belgium, Czechoslovakia, as well as other lands were profound and frequently deeply moving, because he had visited them many times and was thoroughly familiar with their civilization. Japan, however, was different. He had merely skimmed surfaces. His volume on Japan should therefore be looked upon only as a guidebook for tourists who have no knowledge whatsoever of this land of mystery and magic.

In sharp contrast is his work *The New Turkey (La Turquie nouvelle)* (1954), in which Duhamel describes a land with which he is thoroughly familiar. He had studied Turkey's history and culture many years before he visited the country. When he began his volume, he first made mention of the reforms instituted by Kemal Ataturk, "the father of the Turks," as he was known. There was no question but that Duhamel admired Ataturk, whom he considered an extraordinary general and statesman, a man who had commanded an army division during World War I, had been elected president of the provisional Turkish government by the National Assembly (1920), and became the first president of the Turkish Republic (1923). It was Ataturk, Duhamel further noted, who had organized forces to oppose the occupation of Turkey by the Greek army, who had occidentalized this primitive land. From a poor and backward region, Ataturk created a modern country with fine universities and excellent schools. He had also instituted Western teaching techniques, encouraged scientific studies, and seen to the building of new and finely equipped medical schools and hospitals. Industrial progress was also noticeable in the many factories which had cropped up, the roads, the reforesting of land. The Turks, a sturdy lot, worked with enthusiasm on these projects.

Certainly, Turkey would be confronted with all those problems which wracked Occidental civilization. Still, there was a noticeable philosophical difference—and for the better—which he made mention of in his volume. Thirty years previous, when Duhamel had visited Turkey, he had noticed the people were busy, for the most part, contemplating the ruins of a past civilization. Now, however, they were occupied in more positive pursuits: building for the present and for the future. They seemed to be fired with fresh enthusiasm; they worked together, hoping that with each step forward greater prosperity would be in the offing.

Despite the technical and industrial advances—and even the new frame of mind he had noticed in this land—problems would certainly arise to plague such a vista of glory as they envisaged. An imbalance between professional and nonprofessionals would soon occur. Too many people were being trained to follow intellectual professions, Duhamel felt. It is better, he declared, to have one good foreman than a poor lawyer or one intelligent artisan than one more mediocre doctor. Duhamel was anticipating a problem which plagues all modern societies today: the lack of skilled manual labor.

Three years after Duhamel visited Turkey, he set foot on the land of Israel. His fascinating study, *Israel, Key to the Orient (Israël clef de l'Orient)* (1957), resulted. In this volume Duhamel gives a sympathetic and engrossing account of his trip to the land of the Bible. He begins his work, as is his custom, with a brief political history, including the English dominion over the land, the heroic fight for independence and the enormous energy expended by the Zionists and the newly arrived refugees in building their nation.

Duhamel was enormously impressed with the fervor which went into the working of the land: the planting of trees, vegetables, and fruits of all types. The ability of the settlers to work long and arduous hours, their desire for peace and their independent spirit impressed him greatly. The Arabs he saw about him still vegetated in indolence, unwilling or unable to work, to partake of the enormous activity and growth process taking place around them. Duhamel was inspired with sympathy but mostly with pity for their ignorance and filth.

As a patriotic Frenchman, Duhamel felt proud of the fact that France had done so much for Israel, had contributed greatly to its well-being in terms of the military, political, and economic aid it had given. The French ambassador took Duhamel about the land to visit. He showed him the fine roads which were being built at an incredibly rapid pace, a kibbutz in which communal living had proven its fruitfulness. Duhamel noted the similarities between this kind of communal system and the ideal that early Christians had envisaged. The Israelis had, most certainly, been inspired by the Zionist Theodor Herzl, who believed strongly in the establishment of a utopia. They had been fired by his spirit.

Duhamel was particularly drawn to the language situation. The Israelis had revived a language considered for so many years as dead. Now, it had been resurrected and spoken with ease by young and old in Israel. As a doctor, Duhamel also noted with astonishment the extraordinary medical treatment administered in the hospitals, the excellent and wholesome food habits of the Israelis. When he went to visit the University of Jerusalem, to lecture there, he lauded his listeners for their desire to learn. When he visited Haifa, another joy awaited him; the celebrated school, the Technion, had been built by French architects.

Though Duhamel felt deeply about the Israelis and admired their determination and zeal, their enormous skill and will to succeed, he could not but see a road fraught with difficulties ahead for them. Faced with the constant possibility of annihilation, these people were very nearly frenetic in their will to live and to build. He viewed as inevitable the eventual strife between Arabs and Israelis. Another Near East war would be unleashed shortly, he predicted. Nasser, Duhamel was convinced, was a replica of Hitler. One could not, he asserted, deal with this kind of individual on rational grounds. He was convinced that if the Arab countries would help each other rather than seek to distract the populace with the thought of war, they would certainly be better off and would be improving their health and welfare. But Nasser and his henchmen, he noted, were determined to preserve the wealth and power for themselves, at the expense of the masses. If they permitted the masses to starve, they could better foment hatred for Israel, blaming their neighbor for their own problems. The future, Duhamel predicted, was dim for all peace-loving people. He hoped that Israel—courageous, tenacious, and idealistic—would be able to survive as a people and as a nation.

II *Civilization*

Concomitant with Duhamel's travel books was the publication of a series of essays dealing with semiphilosophical topics: modern society, its goals, its mores, and its future. In *Manual of the Protester (Manuel du protestataire)* (1952) he once again takes up a theme he had already sounded out many times before: the notion that the state was becoming too powerful a vehicle in modern society, that it was suffocating all individualism, incentive, and originality. He again voices his distaste for the machine and for the many factories which had done so much to mar the beauties of nature.

In a chapter on "The City of the Future and the Suffering City," Duhamel sees for the future, the formation of a society in which each member will become a living machine, a robot of sorts, trained to perform one and only one well-defined function, incapable, therefore, of reacting in any personal or critical manner to his work or anything surrounding him. In the city of the future, Duhamel declares, "order" will be proclaimed as the rule of the day. Such a goal, in view of the chaotic times in which he was living, could only spell disaster. He had seen what "order" had meant to Germany, a land permeated with such an ideal. This did not mean that Duhamel sought disorder—he always sought a happy medium.

France, he further states, is a fatigued land, in certain respects highly disoriented. Still it is a nation which has maintained a critical outlook upon life, which can still boast of spontaneity and individualism. France has not yet been totally engulfed by "modern" technical civilization, where people and things are devoured so stealthily by the machine. In such a system, individuals, at least sensitive ones, will be immersed in feelings of melancholia, anxiety, and conflict. Their psyches cannot possibly develop at the same rate as the mechanical system. No time will be left for self-probing, for solitude, for inner meditation, for relaxation. People are forever on the go, rarely aware of their state of extreme agitation—of their goals in life.

Duhamel had detected this state of affairs in the United States when he visited it. He had unequivocally condemned America in *America: The Menace, Scenes from the Life of the Future.* When he again stepped on American shores in 1945, he felt quite differently. He expressed his extreme gratitude toward a land and its "great people" who had done so much to help his country.[2] He felt that should another misfortune come to crush the "old European civilization," America would and could help out. During this latest trip to the United

States, Duhamel visited universities, libraries, and museums. He spoke to intellectuals as well as to businessmen. On his first trip, he very nearly deliberately avoided the intelligentsia and dwelled amid the slaughterhouses of Chicago, experiencing America at its worst. Now he was convinced that there was another side to America, that it was not merely the country of material entities, but a fructuous land in which sciences, philosophy, and poetry were burgeoning.

Duhamel nevertheless did warn America, as well as France and other great nations, that medicine should not become a collection or government-run profession. He rejected the idea of the doctor being reduced to the state of an automaton, of his becoming the executor of a "catalogue of impersonal acts." Doctors must at all costs keep contact with the patient and remain free of governmental encroachment. He further decried the fact that general practitioners were slowly disappearing from the face of the world, that specialists had become the rule of the day. Indeed, if medicine continued to become more and more impersonal, a day would come when the patient would call on the phone, give his symptoms to the computer and the proper drugs would be prescribed to him immediately. Automatic medicine, therefore, would be in vogue.

If medicine were to be practiced in this manner, then children too would be taken from their mothers at birth, placed in various institutions, given tests to discover their aptitudes, and would pursue their education accordingly. The child would be sent to the proper school, receive whatever training he would be equipped to perform, and set out on the road of life—computerized. The mother, "rid" of her offspring at a very early age, would be free to work. In such an automated and impersonal world—where would love, emotion, nostalgia, sensitivity, and all the other attributes or qualities of man reside?

In a series of essays written from 1942 to 1954, *Reading, a Refuge (Refuges de la lecture)* (1954), Duhamel offers society, or at least certain individuals who might read his book, an escape from a humdrum and uninspired existence, as well as a positive and creative activity: reading. For Duhamel, there were few activities which could rival the pleasures afforded by books. Such a pastime, to be sure, requires a certain amount of effort on the part of the practitioner, but the joys are immeasurable. Indeed, as contrasted with other activities which require little or no effort on the part of the individual (radio, television, movies), Duhamel felt that reading is the most beneficial. Moreover, it is an excellent discipline, a way of life. The book teaches

one how others have experienced life firsthand, how culture and the
fruits of life have permeated existences. Reading, furthermore,
broadens one's life pattern and ideational attitudes.

Reading offers spiritual food. In this connection, Duhamel hoped
that churches would not further mechanize their offerings. Loud-
speakers introduced in the churches are bad enough, since they
disorient parishioners, preventing them from immersing themselves
totally in the spiritual experience. If church services were to be
recorded, however, transmitted in this way to those in the church as
well as to those at home, the impact of God upon man would be
considerably lessened, perhaps becoming nonexistent. It would then be
possible, Duhamel reasoned, for the Host to be taken by communicants
in their homes, sent to them in steel boxes. On Sunday mornings, for
example, the parishioner would sit in his armchair, in his slippered feet,
enjoying the warmth of his apartment. Then, at the right moment,
when the priest says the necessary word, the Host would be taken.
Religion, conceived of in this fashion, would be totally ineffective and
would be relegated to the role of pill-taking.

Other chapters of interest in this volume deal with history's ancient
heroes: Homer's creatures, Roland, the Crusaders, and others. In each
chapter Duhamel details the personalities of these well-known figures,
pointing to their positive as well as to their destructive influences upon
the societies of their time and on future ones. He also offers a
comparison between their psychological makeup and man's present
outlook. Homer's heroes, Duhamel writes, were brutal, deceiving,
arrogant, and vain, but they were capable of friendship. Does modern
man have such capacities? As for Christ, Duhamel declared, even if he
had been pure invention on man's part, he would be a god nonetheless,
and he would not be any less beautiful or admirable because he would
have been the creation of patient and persevering people, the result of
twenty long centuries of humanity and the ideal representation of a
dream of justice and understanding between peoples.

Reading, a Refuge is a particularly meaningful volume because
within its pages Duhamel not only compares the meaning of social,
spiritual, and literary topics but considers the influences these have had
upon man today. In essays devoted to Ronsard, Flaubert, Rimbaud,
Mallarmé, Verlaine, and others, Duhamel seeks to find a common
denominator between those creators and contemporary man. In the
verses written by these poets, their cries, their sighs, their sufferings,
their solitude always follow a bitter voyage through lands unknown,

where the senses, the mind, and utterly new areas of interest surge
forth, revealing in the process fresh areas of interest and experience.
These writers were innovators; they wrote from within and profoundly,
reaching their depths. For this reason their works took on mythic
proportions. They influenced generations because of the power they
had infused into their *song*.

In *Problems of the Hour (Problèmes de l'heure)* (1957), Duhamel
expresses a growing concern with the French government and its
continuous interference with the individual. Duhamel, as has already
been stated, did not believe in a welfare state, but in the true meaning
of democracy, that is, that people should work as individuals for the
benefit of all.

In former centuries, Duhamel declares, artisans took great satisfaction in the works they created, whether they were shoes or objects of
great beauty. This "just" and "venerable" pride which they manifested
in their work no longer exists.[3] A factory worker today, for example,
who spends eight hours a day on an assembly line, rarely sees the
finished product he has helped construct and if he does, he is totally
unaware of his infinitesimal contribution. Indeed, what he has
accomplished is virtually meaningless. Because he feels no satisfaction,
he becomes irate, and his frustrations are transformed into an
unquenchable appetite for material gain or "matter" of all sorts.
Concomitant with the destruction of individual effort is the fact that
education has also been, in the main, leveled down to a frighteningly
low degree. Everyone today, Duhamel declares, wants an education
regardless of his ability. As a result, a society of "elite" will be formed
and made up of mediocre philosophers, mediocre teachers, and so on.
The elevation of the masses, whose abilities may or may not be
adequate to fill high posts, will create, of necessity, an inferior society.
What is even more frightening, however, is the death of artisans,
farmers, and manual laborers. The lower echelons will become
nonexistent. It must be recalled that not everyone is capable of being a
doctor, a lawyer, a teacher, a mathematician, a philospher.

Culture rests on the effort expended in achieving an education and
in the individual's ability or talent to integrate such information into
his daily living experience. If a state sees to it that all people are
kept—artificially, to be sure—in educational institutions of all types, the
results will be disastrous and the state will, in the long run, suffer utter
collapse.

In recent years the state has encroached upon the individual. Like a cold and calculating monster, it has abolished all incentive, all hope for individual ambition, since everything is *given* to the individual, thereby doing away with the usual impediments or hardships needed to stimulate growth and effort. An impersonal, idle, and mediocre society is certainly going to be the rule of the day if such a trend continues.

Despite the fact that Duhamel found much to castigate in modern society, he was never a defeatist. He was still able to enjoy the beauties in nature as well as those in man. In his daily walking excursions through Paris, in his writings and readings, his friendships and his family ties, he knew happiness. These far outweighed the dissatisfactions he saw in the world. On the contrary, it was because he was so much a part of life, so basically fascinated by its variegated aspects, that he so bitterly criticized what he found to be unpleasant.

In *News of the Somber Empire (Nouvelles du sombre empire)* (1960), a novel in which a hero commits suicide and is, therefore, sent to Gehenna, Duhamel outlines a hell which faintly resembles the world he lived in. Lestrangier, the hero of this fantastic tale, finally discovers that the "hell" in which he is living at present is a replica of his earth life. At the end of the novel, Lestrangier realizes that the entire incident was a bad dream, that he is not dead at all, and that he is very grateful indeed to be alive. Such an attitude could readily sum up Duhamel's view at this period in his life. Though there is much to correct in the world, there is still no greater experience than life itself—and everyone must become aware of this incredibly marvelous gift allotted to men—before it is too late.

Whether Duhamel wrote books on his travels or composed philosophical essays or novels, he was mainly preoccupied with man. As a scientist and doctor, he was asked to write a volume concerning the research work being done on cancer. In *Crusade against Cancer (Croisade contre le cancer)* (1955), he defined this dread disease which Hippocrates, he wrote, had named after the sign of the zodiac, the crab. Duhamel tried to inspire his readers with courage and hope that man, eventually, will find a cure for this life-killer.

From a scientific point of view, Duhamel always kept up with the latest in medicine, and as a literary philosopher he was constantly striving to make life a more pleasurable and fruitful experience. In *Problems of Civilization (Problèmes de civilisation)* (1963), a volume he divided into four sections ("Treatise on Departure," "Fables of My Life," "Medicine in the Twentieth Century," "Problems of Civilization"), he again drew attention to the fact that life is part of a giant and eternal force. Man, he wrote, must partake of life as profoundly as possible; he must cultivate his soul, his mind. Man must be courageous and never fear the future; he must help those who cannot find themselves. Only by drinking deeply of all phases of this existence can one pass into the next, realistically and unperturbed.

One day, perhaps soon, I shall cease to live. My body of flesh will disintegrate, more or less quickly. . . . But I cannot believe that the treasure, which will be my memory, will efface itself into nothingness. My memory gives me, for this reason, the feeling and the hope of spiritual eternity which is my supreme consolation.[4]

CHAPTER 10

Conclusion

D UHAMEL DIED ON April 13, 1966. He had not been well for some time. Because of his failing health he had retired to his country home in the Valmondois (Val d'Oise). There, he felt strengthened and relaxed. The greenery and forest land, still unspoiled by industry and urban expansion, created an atmosphere of well-being.

Duhamel's death put an end to several years of moral suffering. Not only had he witnessed—and helplessly—the splitting, crumbling and disintegration of a world he had known so well, but he also foresaw a third and deadly world holocaust. His sadness was profound.

Duhamel was also pained to learn that he now belonged to a past generation, that he was no longer in tune with the young for whom he had always felt such warmth and such rapport. His books, though still read, were no longer devoured with the same fervor and ardor they had once been. In the 1920's, his works had been best sellers, conversation pieces. In the 1960's, they were looked upon as fine literature, not as indispensable or controversial volumes. His message of good will, of study, of classical education, and of a return to nature fell on deaf ears. He felt most strongly the sting of hurt, the bitterness of misunderstanding, and fear for the future.

Duhamel finally and regretfully accepted the fact that man cannot learn from past mistakes, that each of us has to experience bitterness and sweetness for himself. A man's personality, he concluded, is so filled with turmoil that he is unable to assimilate his swelling feelings of anger and hatred. These, therefore, have to be expelled, leveled at others in some aggressive manner. Then only through violence, man thinks—and erroneously—can equilibrium be achieved.

Duhamel's funeral, which took place on the morning of April 16, 1966, was simple. Liturgical chants and some of Bach's little-known works, which Duhamel so loved, emanated from the village church.

Present at the services were ministers, prefects, generals, governors, representatives of medical and scientific academies, writers of note. All came to honor a man who had done so much for humanity.

Which of Duhamel's works answer a need in society at this time? Which of the many volumes will know eternity?

Certainly, Duhamel's two admirable war books, *The New Book of Martyrs* and *Civilization,* touch upon the deepest of human levels and are meaningful to us today in our war-infested world. The feelings, sensations, anguishes expressed by Duhamel in these works have taken on eternal stature.

The Salavin cycle also takes its rightful place among great works of literature. Duhamel was the *creator* of the Salavin type: the introvert, the *raté,* the one who seeks to be what is not within his capacities to become. Salavin is depicted in depth and so cogently that all those who read the volumes in which he figures can project upon him, can look at themselves, in part at least, through a mirror image.

The Pasquier chronicles are fascinating from a historical point of view. The intimate details of family life at the turn of the century and during World War I are revealed in dramatic and incisive terms. More than a historical piece, however, the Pasquier chronicles deal with eternal themes, such as music, medicine, business, war, and also with elemental problems: the joy a mother experiences when rearing her children, the profound sorrow she knows and the self-abnegating attitude she displays toward a philandering, solipsistic husband, endowed with boundless imagination.

Duhamel's many social and political treatises, such as *America: The Menace, Scenes from the Life of the Future, In Defense of Letters, The Humanist and the Automaton,* to mention but a few, are quite remarkable because of their perceptive nature. Though not alone in predicting man's subservience to the machine, his lack of individuality, Duhamel felt them perhaps more keenly because his love of nature and of humanity was so profound. A doctor, a man who was guided first by the heart and then by the head, could only look with horror at the shocking, bewildering, frighteningly rapid pace of the "March of the Big Steel Machines."

Duhamel's major works fit into our contemporary fad-mad, psychedelic world mainly as counterweights. He is a representative of the heart, of feeling, understanding, balance, harmony, and stability. These character traits are so submerged in today's violent, ebullient, ruthless society as to be virtually nonexistent. One gazes at Duhamel's works, therefore, with a twinge of nostalgia, longing, and melancholy—as though one were looking back toward a world that was, not forward to the gaping abyss which awaits us—so similar in nature to the crater into which Empedocles hurled himself in his frantic desire for self-destruction.

Notes and References

Chapter One

1. Georges Duhamel, *Lumières sur ma vie, Biographie de mes fantômes*, II, p. 144.
2. *Ibid*, I, *Inventaire de l'abîme*, p. 49.
3. *Ibid.*, p. 50.
4. *Ibid.*, p. 71.
5. Georges Duhamel, "J. S. Bach: My Companion and Guide," *Musical Opinion* (July, 1950), p. 575.
6. Herbert Antcliffe, "Georges Duhamel on Music," *The Chesterian*, p. 76.
7. Georges Duhamel, *Lumières sur ma vie*, I, p. 230.
8. *Ibid.*, p. 235.
9. *Ibid.*, II, p. 29.
10. *Ibid.*, II, p. 41.
11. *Georges Duhamel*, Editions de la Revue *Le Capitole* (Paris, 1927), p. 70.
12. Georges Duhamel, *Lumières sur ma vie, Le Temps de la recherche*, III, p. 181.
13. Georges Duhamel, *Paul Claudel*, p. 6.
14. *Ibid.*, p. 21.
15. *Ibid.*, p. 50.
16. *Ibid.*, p. 29.
17. Georges Duhamel, *L'Homme en tête*, p. 102.

Chapter Two

1. Georges Duhamel, *Lumières sur ma vie, Le Temps de la recherche*, III, p. 168.
2. *Ibid.*, p. 159.
3. Bettina Knapp, *Louis Jouvet Man of the Theatre*, Columbia University Press, 1957, pp. 8–9.
4. *Georges Duhamel*, III, p. 168.
5. *Georges Duhamel*, Editions de la Revue *Le Capitole*, p. 19.
6. Georges Duhamel, III, p. 205.
7. "Georges Duhamel," *de la Revue Le Capitole*, p. 23.

8. Georges Duhamel, III, p. 206.

9. André Boll, *Jacques Rouché*, Editions de Noël, 1937, p. 19.

10. Bettina Knapp, *Louis Jouvet Man of the Theatre*, pp. 22–28.

11. Maurice Kurtz, *Jacques Copeau*, Nagel, 1950, p. 101.

12. Georges Duhamel, *Lumières sur ma vie, Les Espoirs et les épreuves*, V, p. 99.

13. *Georges Duhamel*, Editions de la Revue *Le Capitole*, p. 19.

14. Georges Duhamel, *Lettres d'Auspasie*, p. 107.

Chapter Three

1. Georges Duhamel, *Lumières sur ma vie, Le Temps de la recherche*, III, p. 242.

2. Georges Duhamel, *Vie des martyrs*, p. 6.

3. *Ibid.*, p. 13.

4. *Ibid.*, p. 45.

5. *Civilisation*, p. 40.

6. *Ibid.*, p. 45.

7. *Ibid.*, p. 47.

8. *Ibid.* p. 22.

9. *Ibid.*, p. 11.

10. Georges Duhamel, *Entretiens dans le tumulte*, p. 18.

11. Georges Duhamel, *La Possession du monde*, p. 34.

12. *Ibid.*, p. 36.

13. *Ibid.*, p. 245.

Chapter Four

1. Georges Duhamel, *Lumières sur ma vie, Le Temps de la recherche*, III, p. 234.

2. Georges Duhamel, *Semailles au vent*, p. 23.

3. Georges Duhamel, *Confession de minuit*, p. 97.

4. *Ibid.*, p. 10.

5. *Ibid.*, p. 28.

6. *Ibid.*, p. 45.

7. Georges Duhamel, *Inventaire de l'abime*, I, p. 34.

8. Georges Duhamel, *Journal de Salavin*, p. 7.

9. *Ibid.*, p. 11.

10. *Ibid.*, p. 34.

11. *Ibid.*, p. 50.

12. *Ibid.*, p. 57.

13. *Ibid.*, p. 207.

14. Georges Duhamel, *Le Club des Lyonnais*, p. 260.

15. *Ibid.*, p. 49.

16. Georges Duhamel, *Tel qu'en lui-même*, p. 241.

17. *Ibid.*, p. 247.

Chapter Five

1. Georges Duhamel, *Remarques sur les mémoires imaginaires*, p. 14.

2. Georges Duhamel, *Les Hommes abandonnés*, p. 104.

3. The other stories in this volume are: "On ne saurait tout dire" "Le Bengali," "Une expédition," "La chambre de l'horloge," "Nouvelle rencontre de Salavin." This entire volume was again published in 1938 by Duhamel with an additional story, "Le dernier voyage de Candide."

4. Georges Duhamel, *Remarques sur les mémoires imaginaires*, p. 64.

5. *Ibid.*, p. 87.

6. Georges Duhamel, *La Pierre d'Horeb*, p. 9.

7. Georges Duhamel, *La Nuit d'Orage*, p. 13.

8. These chapters were reprinted in 1926 under the title *Lettres au Patagon*. Duhamel also included three more essays in this volume: "Sur les amateurs," "Sur les malades," "Sur quelques aventures de l'esprit."

9. The essay "On the Theater" is discussed in Chapter 2, devoted to the theater.

10. Georges Duhamel, *Scènes de la vie future*, p. 231.

11. *Ibid.*, p. 140.

12. *Ibid.*, p. 102.

13. *Ibid.*, p. 58.

14. Georges Duhamel, *Querelle de famille*, p. 8.

15. Georges Duhamel, *L'Humaniste et l'automate*, p. 186.

16. Georges Duhamel, *Chant du Nord*, p. 278.

17. *Ibid.*, p. 80.

18. Georges Duhamel, *Les Plaisirs et les jeux*, p. 46.

19. Georges Duhamel, *Les Erispaudants*, p. 17.

20. *Ibid.*, p. 14.

21. Herbert Antcliffe, "Georges Duhamel on Music," *The Chesterian*, p. 77.

22. *Ibid.*, p. 77.

23. Georges Duhamel, "J. S. Bach: My Companion and Guide," *Musical Opinion* (July, 1950), p. 576.

Chapter Six

1. Georges Duhamel, *Le Jardin des bêtes sauvages*, p. 45.

2. *Ibid.*

3. Georges Duhamel, *Vue de la terre promise*, p. 239.

4. Georges Duhamel, *La Nuit de la Saint-Jean*, p. 29.

5. *Ibid.*, p. 216.

6. Georges Duhamel, *Le Désert de Bièvres*, p. 37.

7. Georges Duhamel, *Les Maîtres*, p. 37.
8. Georges Duhamel, *Cécile parmi nous*, p. 8.
9. *Ibid.*, p. 180.

Chapter Seven

1. Georges Duhamel, *Défense des lettres*, p. 216.
2. Georges Duhamel, *Fables de mon jardin*, p. 81.
3. *Ibid.*, p. 25.
4. *Ibid.*, p. 87.
5. Georges Duhamel, *La Guerre blanche*, p. 80.
6. Georges Duhamel, *Positions françaises*, p. 49.
7. Georges Duhamel, *Lieu d'asile*, p. 142.
8. Georges Duhamel, *Tribulations de l'espérance*, p. 7.
9. Georges Duhamel, *Souvenirs de la vie du paradis*, p. 8.
10. Georges Duhamel, *Le Bestiaire et l'herbier*, p. 89.

Chapter Eight

1. Georges Duhamel, *Le Complexe de Théophile*, p. 225.
2. Georges Duhamel, *Le Voyage de Patrice Périot*, p. 2.
3. *Ibid.*, p. 13.
4. *Ibid.*, p. 255.
5. Georges Duhamel, *Cri des profondeurs*, p. 24.
6. *Ibid.*, p. 166.
7. *Ibid.*, p. 213.
8. *Ibid.*, p. 238.
9. *Ibid.*, p. 246.
10. *Ibid.*, p. 132.
11. Georges Duhamel, *L'Archange de l'aventure*, p. 73.
12. Georges Duhamel, *Les Compagnons de l'Apocalypse*, p. 51.
13. *Ibid.*, p. 229.
14. *Ibid.*, p. 242.
15. *Ibid.*, p. 243.
16. Georges Duhamel, *Le Complexe de Théophile*, p. 13.
17. *Ibid.*, pp. 76–77.
18. *Ibid.*, p. 55.
19. *Ibid.*, p. 86.
20. *Ibid.*
21. *Ibid.*, p. 138.
22. *Ibid.*, p. 204.
23. *Ibid.*

Chapter Nine

1. Georges Duhamel, *Refuges de la lecture*, p. 239.
2. Georges Duhamel, *Manuel du protestataire*, p. 117.
3. Georges Duhamel, *Problèmes de l'heure*, p. 23.
4. Georges Duhamel, *Problèmes de civilisation*, p. 227.

Selected Bibliography

PRIMARY SOURCES

I. *Fiction:*

L'Archange de l'aventure, Mercure de France, 1956.
Chronique des Pasquier
    Le Notaire du Havre, Mercure de France, 1933.
    Le Jardin des bêtes sauvages, Mercure de France, 1934.
    Vue de la terre promise, Mercure de France, 1934.
    La Nuit de la Saint-Jean, Mercure de France, 1935.
    Le Désert de Bièvres, Mercure de France, 1937.
    Les Maîtres, Mercure de France, 1937.
    Cécile parmi nous, Mercure de France, 1938.
    Le Combat contre les ombres, Mercure de France, 1939.
    Suzanne et les jeunes hommes, Mercure de France, 1941.
    La Passion de Joseph Pasquier, Montreal: Editions de l'Arbre, 1944.
Les Compagnons de l'Apocalypse, Mercure de France, 1956.
Le Complexe de Théophile, Mercure de France, 1958.
Cri des profondeurs, Mercure de France, 1951.
Le Dernier voyage de Candide, Fernand Sorlot, 1938.
Les Erispaudants, Société de gravure sur bois originale, 1926.
Les Hommes abandonnés, Mercure de France, 1921.
Nouvelles du sombre empire, Mercure de France, 1960.
La Nuit d'Orage, Mercure de France, 1928.
La Pierre d'Horeb, Mercure de France, 1926.
Le Prince de Jaffar, Mercure de France, 1924.
Souvenirs de la vie du paradis, Mercure de France, 1946.
Vie et aventures de Salavin.
    Confession de minuit, Mercure de France, 1920.
    Deux hommes, Mercure de France, 1924.
    Journal de Salavin, Mercure de France, 1927.
    Le Club des Lyonnais, Mercure de France, 1929.
    Tel qu'en lui-même, Mercure de France, 1932.

Le Voyage de Patrice Périot, Mercure de France, 1950.
Les Voyageurs de l'Espérance, Librairie Gedalge, 1953.

II. *Drama:*

Le Combat, Mercure de France, 1913.
Dans l'ombre des statues, Nouvelle revue française, 1912.
La Journée des aveux, Mercure de France, 1924.
La Lumière, Eugène Figuière, 1911.
L'Oeuvre des athlètes suivi de Lapointe et Ropiteau, Nouvelle revue française, 1920.

III. *Poetry:*

Anthologie de la poésie lyrique française de la fin du XVe siècle à la fin du XIXe siècle, Leipzig: Insel-Verlag, 1923.
Ballades, Les Ecrivains réunis, 1926.
Compagnons 1910–1912, Nouvelles revue française, 1912.
Des Légendes, des batailles, Editions de "L'Abbaye," 1907.
Elégies, Block, 1920
L'Homme en tête, Editions "Vers et Prose," 1909.
Selon ma loi, Eugène Figuière, 1910.

IV. *Essays:*

L'Alsace entrevue ou l'aveugle et le paralytique (Berthold Mahn collaborated with Duhamel on this work). Strasbourg: Librairie de la Mesange, 1931.
Au Chevet de la civilisation, Flammarion, 1938.
Chronique des saisons amères, 1940–1943, Paul Hartmann, 1944.
Civilisation française, Hachette, 1944.
Les Confessions sans pénitence, Plon, 1941.
Consultation aux pays d'Islam, Mercure de France, 1947.
Défense des lettres, Mercure de France, 1937.
Déliberations, Les Cahiers de Paris, 1925.
Deux patrons, Paul Hartmann, 1937.
Discours aux nuages, Editions du siècle, 1934.
Discours de reception de M. Georges Duhamel à l'Académie française, Mercure de France, 1936.
Entretiens dans le tumulte, Mercure de France, 1919.
Entretien sur l'esprit européen, Aux éditions des cahiers libres, 1928.
Essai sur le roman, Marcelle Lesage, 1925.
Essai sur une renaissance dramatique, Lapina, 1926.
Géographie cordiale de l'Europe, Mercure de France, 1931.
Guerre et littérature, A. Monnier, 1920.

Henry de Varoquier, L'Art d'aujourd'hui, 1925.
Homère au XXe siècle, Union latine d'édition, 1947.
L'Humaniste et l'automate, Paul Hartmann, 1933.
Israël, clef de l'Orient, Mercure de France, 1957.
Le Japon, Mercure de France, 1953.
Les Jumeaux de Vallangoujard, Paul Hartmann, 1931.
Lettres au Patagon, Mercure de France, 1926.
Lieu d'asile, Mercure de France, 1940.
Manuel du protestataire, Mercure de France, 1952.
Maurice de Vlaminck, Les Ecrivains réunis, 1927.
Mémorial de la guerre blanche, 1938, Mercure de France, 1939.
La Musique consolatrice, Monaco: Editions du Rocher, 1944.
La Musique libératrice, Editions des fêtes du peuple, 1921.
Notes sur la technique poétique (with Charles Vildrac), Chez les
    librairies et chez les auteurs, 1910.
Pages de mon carnet, Editions des cahiers libres, 1931.
Paroles de médecin, Monaco: Editions du Rocher, 1946.
Paul Claudel, Mercure de France, 1913.
Les Poètes et la poésie, 1912–1913, Mercure de France, 1915.
Positions françaises, Mercure de France, 1940.
La Possession du monde, Mercure de France, 1919.
Problèmes de civilisation, Mercure de France, 1963.
Propos critiques, première série. Eugène Figuière, 1912.
Querelle de famille, Mercure de France, 1932.
Refuges de la lecture, Mercure de France, 1954.
Remarques sur les mémoires imaginaires, Mercure de France, 1934.
Scènes de la vie future, Mercure de France, 1930.
Semailles au vent, Monaco: Editions du Rocher, 1947.
Travail, ô mon seul repos, Mercure de France, 1959.
Tribulations de l'espérance, Mercure de France, 1947.
La Turquie nouvelle, Mercure de France, 1954.
Vie des Martyrs, Mercure de France, 1917.
Le Voyage de Moscou, Mercure de France, 1927.

V. *Other Prose:*

Civilisation 1914–1917 (pseudonym, Denis Thévenin), Mercure de
    France, 1918.
Fables de mon jardin, Mercure de France, 1936.
Lumières sur ma vie
       Inventaire de l'abîme, Paul Hartmann, 1944.
       Biographie de mes fantômes, Paul Hartmann, 1944.
       Le Temps de la recherche, Paul Hartmann, 1947.
       La Pesée des âmes, Mercure de France, 1949.
       Les Espoirs et les épreuves, Mercure de France, 1953.

Mon Royaume, Paul Hartmann, 1932.
Les Plaisirs et les jeux, Mercure de France, 1922.

SECONDARY SOURCES

Articles on Georges Duhamel:

ANTCLIFFE, HERBERT. "Georges Duhamel on Music," *The Chesterian,* Vol. XIX, 1938.
SYLVESTRE, GUY. "Georges Duhamel et la musique," *Revue de l'Université d'Ottawa.* Jan.–March, 1945.

Books on Duhamel:

ANTOINE, ANDRÉ. *Georges Duhamel.* Editions de la Revue *Le Capitole.* Paris, 1927.
DURTAIN, LUC. *Georges Duhamel, L'homme et l'oeuvre.* Paris: Les Cahiers des amis des livres, 1920. A penetrating study by a friend.
FALLS, WILLIAM. *Le Message humain de Georges Duhamel.* Paris: Boivin, 1948.
HUMBOURG, PIERRE. *Georges Duhamel et son oeuvre.* Paris: Editions de la Nouvelle Revue Critique, 1930. A fine analysis.
KEATING, CLARK. L. *Critic of Civilization.* Lexington: University of Kentucky Press, 1965. An excellent appraisal of Duhamel, the man and his work.
MONDOR, HENRI. *Lettres et images pour Georges Duhamel.* Paris: Gallimard, 1937. Very helpful work.
SANTELLI, CÉSAR. *Georges Duhamel.* Paris: Mercure de France, 1927.
———. *Georges Duhamel, L'homme et l'oeuvre.* Paris: Bordas, 1947. Two excellent works.
SAURIN, MARCEL. *Les Ecrits de Georges Duhamel.* Paris: Mercure de France, 1951. Valuable bibliography of Duhamel's works.
SENECHAL, CHRISTIAN. *L'Abbaye de Créteil.* Paris: André Delpuech, 1951. Excellent study.
SIMON, PIERRE-HENRI. *Georges Duhamel.* Paris: Les Editions du Temps Present, 1946. Thorough and imaginative appraisal.
TERISSE, ANDRÉ. *Georges Duhamel.* Paris: Fernand Nathan, 1951. Very well done.
THERIVE, ANDRÉ. *Georges Duhamel ou l'intelligence du coeur.* Paris: Rasmussen, 1925. A nostalgic work.

Index